ROYAL AIR FORCE

Published in association with Royal Air Force Media and Communications, Headquarters Air Command

EDITORIAL
Editor: Paul E Eden
Group Editor: Nigel Price

DESIGN
Studio Manager: Steve Donovan
Design: Tracey Croft, Andy O'Neil, Dominique Maynard, Dave Robinson, Tom Bagley

PRODUCTION
Production Manager: Janet Watkins

ADVERTISING and MARKETING
Senior Advertisement Manager: Ian Maxwell
Advertising Group Manager: Brodie Baxter
Advertising Production Manager: Debi McGowan
Group Marketing Manager: Martin Steele
Marketing: Shaun Binnington, Amy Donkersley

COMMERCIAL DIRECTOR: Ann Saundry
PUBLISHER and MANAGING DIRECTOR: Adrian Cox
EXECUTIVE CHAIRMAN: Richard Cox

CONTACTS
Key Publishing Ltd
PO Box 100, Stamford,
Lincolnshire, PE9 1XQ, UK
Tel: 01780 755131
Fax: 01780 757261
E-mail : enquiries@keypublishing.com
www.keypublishing.com

DISTRIBUTION
Seymour Distribution Ltd
2 Poultry Avenue, London EC1A 9PP
020 7429 400

PRINTED BY
Warners (Midlands) plc, The Maltings, Bourne, Lincs PE10 9PH

PUBLISHER
Key Publishing Ltd
PRINTED IN ENGLAND

Cover image: **Typhoon** represents the cutting edge of RAF airpower. Jamie Hunter/ Aviacom

Foreword

In 2018, the Royal Air Force will be 100 years old. Over a century of operations it has inspired and employed technology at the cutting edge of possibility, developed tactics and procedures that have astounded – and defeated – the very best air arms, and fostered personnel of immense courage, personality and talent.

Of course, it is the Service's aircraft that inevitably grab the attention of media and public alike, the Royal Air Force performing to the highest standards in roles that cover the entire gamut of modern airpower. And these are roles practised and perfected in action, since the RAF has been engaged in Coalition warfare since Operation Granby, the Gulf war of 1991.

The Tornado, in particular, has been on the frontline for more than 25 years, even as new technologies transformed it from the GR.Mk 1 'bomber' of 1991 into the GR.Mk 4 precision attack platform that is today at the peak of its capability. Also combat proven, Typhoon is set to take on all Tornado's air-to-ground capability during 2018, adding to its own formidable air-to-air prowess.

Without intelligence and support, however, fast jet airpower is as nothing. Voyager, the RAF's new tanker/transport aircraft, is delivering outstanding service, refuelling Tornados and Typhoons, as well as Coalition aircraft operating over Iraq and Syria. At the same time, Voyager provides essential support to UK and Falkland Islands air defence, as well as moving personnel globally.

And while the huge C-17 strategic airlifter and Hercules tactical transport continue in their long-established roles, the new A400M Atlas is realising its full range of mission capability. Together, Atlas, Voyager, C-17 and Hercules represent an RAF transport and tanker fleet perhaps more capable than at any time in the past.

Underpinning government and UK Defence decision making, Intelligence, Surveillance, Target Acquisition and Reconnaissance has combined disciplines with origins earlier than those of the Royal Air Force itself. With its Airseeker, Sentinel, Sentry, Shadow and Reaper aircraft, the Service gathers data from across the intelligence spectrum, informing targeting decisions and influencing policy at the highest levels.

Through a mix of new and upgraded aircraft, and a range of precision-guided weapons, the Royal Air Force delivers world-class combat capability. But it also fulfils essential humanitarian roles at home and overseas. The upgraded Puma and Chinook fleets are as effective at delivering humanitarian aid as they are over the battlefield. Both are air deployable by C-17 and Atlas, enabling vertical lift to reach disaster zones anywhere in the world in a matter of hours. They are also on call should the UK find itself in crisis; few who saw the TV footage will forget the RAF Chinook crew moving bags of sand into a massive breech in the banks of the River Douglas at Croston, Lancashire in the last days of 2016.

In the near future, the Royal Air Force is looking forward to returning to the maritime role with a force of brand new P-8A Poseidon anti-submarine and maritime patrol aircraft. The F-35B Lightning is more imminent, with the first UK-based examples expected to land at RAF Marham next year.

As the RAF's first stealthy aircraft, the Lightning introduces an entirely new capability, while its advanced sensor suite is likely to revolutionise the way the Service does business. It will also see the RAF and Fleet Air Arm take UK fast air back to sea as it embarks in HMS *Queen Elizabeth II* from 2020.

With the latest technologies on the frontline, it is imperative the RAF lays the foundations of its aircrew training in a similarly high-tech manner. The future of military flying training has been invested in the UK Military Flying Training System, which will see a fleet of new glass-cockpit training aircraft enter service and begin teaching students by 2019.

These are exciting times for the Royal Air Force, with new aircraft types and emerging capabilities to the fore. Never before has the Service so exemplified its key virtues of agility, adaptability and capability.

Paul E Eden

Representing the cutting-edge of fast jet training, the forward cockpit of the Hawk T2 is optimised for students going on to the Typhoon and, in the very near future, Lightning. Paul Heasman

Typhoon continues to evolve into a true multi-role platform, as adept in air fighting as it is at ground attack.
Sgt Peter George/© UK MoD Crown Copyright 2017

Royal Air Force
Aircraft

Guaranteeing the safety of our skies, prosecuting terrorist targets with deadly precision, gathering intelligence of national and international importance, moving heavy equipment and personnel across the world at a moment's notice, and repairing breached river banks, saving communities on the brink from inundation… all these tasks and more constitute the regular routine of Royal Air Force operations. Alongside its exceptional people, the Service relies on a revitalised and varied fleet of fixed-wing aircraft and helicopters to deliver effect wherever and whenever required by UK government.

Administratively, RAF aircraft are primarily organised under Nos 1, 2 and 22 Groups, taking responsibility for air combat, air combat support and training, respectively. Within these Groups, aircraft fleets are arranged by type and/or role into Forces, the exception being

Chinook Force and Puma Force, under Support Helicopter Force, which come under the control of Joint Helicopter Command (JHC), a tri-service organisation, rather than an RAF Group.

1 GROUP

Perhaps most obviously through reporting online, on our television screens and in the press, 1 Group includes Tornado Force, Typhoon Force and the nascent Lightning Force; less obviously, it also manages ISTAR Force, a concentration of the RAF's mixed Intelligence, Surveillance, Target Acquisition and Reconnaissance fleet, which also takes data from the Litening III targeting pods carried into combat by Tornado and Typhoon, and the Reconnaissance Airborne Pod Tornado (RAPTOR) system.

Tornado has been deployed on combat operations continuously since 1991, yet represents a globally unique capability. With its

out of service date (OSD) set for 2019, Project Centurion is under way to transfer its Brimstone and Storm Shadow weapons and other capability onto Typhoon, the Paveway IV GPS/laser-guided bomb having already appeared on the more modern jet.

Today's combat aircraft are designed for a lifetime of upgrade and Typhoon is no exception. Already a world class air defender, its capability will be expanded with the Meteor air-to-air missile in 2018, followed closely by Brimstone and Storm Shadow, delivering true multi-role capability in one aircraft. Meanwhile, Lightning is scheduled to begin the move into its RAF Marham home next year, introducing not only a dramatic new type into 1 Group's inventory, but also an entirely new capability.

ISTAR Force is unusual in comprising multiple aircraft types. Airseeker, Sentinel, Sentry and Shadow are all based at RAF Waddington, but

Aircraft Designation

Royal Air Force aircraft are traditionally given a name, followed by a role designator and mark number. The Hawk T.Mk 2, for example, is designated with a 'T' for training and is the second mark of Hawk, ie Mark 2, or Mk 2. Many variations in presentation exist, even within official documents, but here the above style has been used as the full, formal designation system. In general use, designations are usually shortened to name, role designator and mark number, as Hawk T2, for example. This less formal style is also used here, better reflecting service use and providing a little variety for the reader.

When aircraft were acquired from US manufacturers, their US military designations were rarely adopted in the past, but some are known equally by their US and UK designations – the E-3D, formally Sentry AEW.Mk 1, is a prime example. Other types, including the C-17, which was originally acquired on lease, have never received formal UK designations.

deploy for long periods. The Reaper remotely piloted air system (RPAS) also falls under ISTAR Force, but the aircraft are based in theatre and their controlling squadrons at Creech Air Force Base, Nevada and Waddington.

2 GROUP

With the bulk of its fleet stationed at RAF Brize Norton, 2 Group has undergone a period of transformation, replacing old equipment with the latest and most capable designs. Voyager is providing exceptional service as an air-to-air refuelling tanker, deployed for Operation Shader, but also supporting quick reaction alert (QRA) Typhoons and other assets on the Falkland Islands and over the UK. It has also

revolutionised the RAF's ability to move troops and personnel efficiently and in comfort.

Strategic and tactical airlift remain the primary responsibilities of the C-17 and Hercules Forces, respectively, but the new A400M Atlas is already taking on strategic responsibilities even as its tactical capabilities continue to expand. In the same way that Lightning will bring a new capability to 1 Group, so Atlas brings dramatic change to 2 Group, delivering a mix of strategic and high-end tactical airlift in one platform.

Away from Brize Norton, 2 Group also contains 32 (The Royal) Squadron, stationed at RAF Northolt. Tasked in the Command Support Air Transport role, 32(TR) Sqn is unique as the RAF's only operator of fixed and rotary-wing equipment, with two 146 variants and the GrandPower helicopter on strength.

SUPPORT HELICOPTERS

The Chinook and Puma Forces have seen dramatic changes in capability in recent years. Project Julius has retrofitted a new Thales glass cockpit into legacy Chinook HC.Mk 2 and 3 helicopters, creating the Mk 4 and 5, respectively, while new-build HC.Mk 6 helicopters have entered service, uniquely equipped with the same flight deck. Further changes are planned and Chinook Force continues to expand in capability.

Puma Force has been transformed by a far-reaching upgrade to Puma HC.Mk 2 standard, which ironically leaves the aircraft virtually identical to its Mk 1 predecessor externally. Internally the helicopter is transformed, however, with new engines and avionics, a glass cockpit and increased fuel capacity.

Both Support Helicopter types fall under Joint Helicopter Command, where they operate alongside Army Air Corps Apache and new-generation Wildcat helicopters, and the

Role Designators

Designator	Role
AEW	Airborne Early Warning
C	Transport
CC	Communications Transport
FGR	Fighter, Ground-Attack, Reconnaissance
GR	Ground-Attack, Reconnaissance
HC	Helicopter Transport
HT	Helicopter Training
KC	Tanker Transport
R	Reconnaissance
T	Training

Watchkeeper RPAS, and Fleet Air Arm Merlin HC.Mk 3 and Wildcat aircraft.

22 GROUP

A high-tech frontline counts for little without a modern training fleet capable of fully preparing future aircrew for the latest operational equipment. The UK Military Flying Training System (UK MFTS) is already transforming flying training for all three forces and falls under the jurisdiction of 22 Group. With the BAE Systems Hawk T.Mk 2 advanced fast jet trainer well established in service, and the Prefect and Texan II imminent, UK fast jet training will soon be accomplished from first flight to graduation in a glass cockpit.

Likewise, from 2019, multi-engine students will progress through Prefect to Phenom and then on to their operational conversion unit for another all-glass training programme. A similar story is being written at the Defence Helicopter Flying School, where the latest generation Juno and Jupiter helicopters are replacing the Squirrel and Griffin, after many years of faithful service. ●

Left: **Typhoons from II(AC) Sqn (foreground) and 6 Sqn represent the cutting edge of RAF airpower. The type's primary responsibility is the air defence of the UK and Falkland Islands, but it also has a crucial precision attack role in Operation Shader.** Jamie Hunter/Aviacom

Right: **With the powerful Chinook, the RAF delivers an altogether different form of airpower to the Typhoon's. Working closely with the British Army, the Chinook and Puma provide essential battlefield mobility.** Cpl Rob Travis/© UK MoD Crown Copyright 2017

British Aerospace 146

ROLE:
Exclusively operated out of RAF Northolt by 32 (The Royal) Squadron, the BAe 146 is primarily tasked in the Command Support Air Transport (CSAT) role. Two 146 variants are operational, the VIP-configured CC.Mk 2 and the Quick Change (QC) C.Mk 3, which can be rapidly converted between passenger and cargo configurations.

The CC2's primary role is the transport of senior government ministers and Ministry of Defence (MOD) personnel and, most famously, senior members of the Royal Family, although this work represents by far the minority of 32(TR) Sqn's tasking. If required, the 146's defensive aids suite (DAS) also offers government ministers and high-ranking military leaders protection during visits overseas where a risk to security is perceived.

Outside VIP work, the CC.Mk 2 has an operational role in-theatre, providing essential support to military commanders by moving personnel and smaller freight items. The type's presence also enables key face-to-face engagement between commanders and their personnel, coalition partners and host nation leadership representatives.

Purchased as a pair of ex-TNT 146-200QC aircraft in 2012, the C.Mk 3s entered service in 2013 after modifications, including the addition of a DAS, for RAF service. They have made a considerable contribution to tactical airlift capability, taking on missions that might otherwise have taken larger aircraft off their primary tasking.

CAPABILITY:
The BAe 146 is a quiet, rugged, self-sufficient aircraft equipped with comprehensive back-up systems. This enables it to operate away from base for long periods with little external support. The CC2 is extremely versatile, with excellent short-field performance, good 'hot-and-high' airfield capability (operating off hot climate/high altitude runways), and has the ability to fly from semi-prepared landing strips.

The C3 retains the 10ft 11in × 6ft 4in (3.33 × 1.93m) rear-fuselage freight door of the civilian QC model, providing for convenient loading of palletised freight. Alternatively, palletised passenger seats may be rapidly installed. Thanks to their similarity, crews operate either 146 variant.

TYPE HISTORY:
Hawker Siddeley announced plans to develop the four-engined HS146 airliner in August 1973. It was envisaged as an unusual machine from the outset, employing relatively low powered turbofans and offering exceptional field performance over short routes. With the UK economy declining soon after the announcement, however, work continued only at a trickle, before Hawker Siddeley was absorbed into the nationalised British Aerospace (BAe) in 1977.

On July 10, 1978, BAe announced its decision to proceed with a full 146 programme, rolling out the first BAe 146-100 prototype on May 20, 1981. Designed for a maximum of 93 passengers, the Series 100 flew for the first time on September 3, 1981 and completed its first revenue service, with Dan-Air, on May 27, 1983. In June of that year, two leased 146-100s temporarily joined the ranks at RAF Brize Norton. Designated 146 CC.Mk 1, they evaluated the type as a possible replacement for the Andover turboprops then in service with The Queen's Flight.

Meanwhile, BAe was busy producing the lengthened 146-200, which sacrificed some of the -100's airfield capability for additional capacity, and the longer-still 146-300. Quiet Trader variants of all three models were available, while availability of the Quick Change convertible variants of the 146-200QT and -300QT was announced in 1988.

One of two BAe 146 CC.Mk 2 CSAT aircraft in service with No. 32(TR) Sqn at RAF Northolt. The special marking on the fin was applied for the unit's centenary in 2016. Cpl Ben Tritta/© UK MoD Crown Copyright 2017

Specification

BAe 146 CC.Mk 2	
Powerplant	four 6,970lb st (31kN) Honeywell ALF502R-5 turbofans
Length	85ft 11½in (26.19m)
Height	28ft 3in (8.61m)
Wingspan	86ft 5in (26.34m)
Wing area	832sqft (77.29m²)
Maximum take-off weight	84,000lb (38,102kg)
Cruising speed at 30,000ft	around 380kt (709km/h)
Typical range	1,400nm (2,593km)
Typical cruising altitude	30,000ft
BAe 146 C.Mk 3	
As CC.Mk 2 except:	
Length	93ft 10in (28.60m)
Typical range	1,200nm (2,222km)

The 146 C.Mk 3 is immediately identifiable by its grey colour scheme, in dramatic contrast to the patriotic finish of the CC.Mk 2. SAC Matt Baker/© UK MoD Crown Copyright 2017

BAe also offered the Statesman VIP version of all three base models and it was this, applied to the 146-100, that formed the basis of an initial order for two 146 CC.Mk 2 aircraft, the first of them delivered to the RAF in April 1986. A third machine was ordered in 1989, but one of the three was sold in 2002.

During the early 1990s, BAe reinvented the 146 as the Avro RJ series of regional airliners. These, and the original design, achieved considerable commercial success and remain in widespread service. ●

Above: **Unusual in configuration, the 146 has a high-set wing, rugged, short undercarriage and T-tail.** Cpl Ben Tritta/© UK MoD Crown Copyright 2017

Service Variants

Designation	First Delivery	Status
146 CC.Mk 2	April 1986	Operational
146 C.Mk 3	2013	Operational

Service Operators

Unit	Type	First Delivery
32(TR) Sqn	146 CC.Mk 2	April 1986
32(TR) Sqn	146 C.Mk 3	2013

The A400M's TP400 turboprops are configured so the outboard engine on each side rotates inwards and the inboard engine outwards, negating their considerable torque and vastly improving the aircraft's handling and performance.
Paul Crouch/© UK MoD Crown Copyright 2017

ROLE: Entering operational service with the Royal Air Force in 2014, Atlas provides tactical airlift and strategic oversize lift capabilities complementing those of the Hercules and C-17 fleets.

CAPABILITY: Atlas has the ability to carry a 25-tonne payload over 2,000nm to established and remote civilian and military airfields, and short unprepared or semi-prepared strips. Capable of operating at altitudes up to 40,000ft, Atlas also

400

ROYAL AIR FORCE

Airbus Defence and Space
A400M Atlas

offers impressive low-level capability. It will accommodate as many as 116 fully-equipped troops; vehicles; helicopters, including a Chinook; mixed loads, including nine aircraft pallets and 54 passengers, or combinations of vehicles, pallets and personnel, up to a payload of 37 tonnes.

Loads are delivered by parachute, gravity extraction from the aircraft's rear ramp (influenced by the cargo's own weight), or by landing. Paratroops will be dropped from the aircraft's dedicated paratroop doors, or from the rear ramp. The Atlas is operated by two pilots and a Weapons Systems Operator (Crewman) (WSOp (Cmn)).

TYPE HISTORY: In 1982, France's Aerospatiale, British Aerospace, West Germany's Messerschmitt-Bölkow-Blohm (MBB) and Lockheed in the US, established the Future International Military Airlifter (FIMA) group to define and develop a replacement for the Lockheed C-130 Hercules and Transall C.160 in wide scale service. Little progress was made as industrial and political differences complicated the group's intentions and in 1989 Lockheed withdrew, ultimately to develop the C-130J Hercules, now in RAF service as the Hercules C4 and C5.

Italy's Alenia and Spain's CASA subsequently joined Aerospatiale, BAe and Deutsche Aerospace (DASA, which had bought MBB in 1989), creating the European Future Large Aircraft (FLA) Group (Euroflag) on June 17, 1991. Work to define the FLA requirement continued as DASA became first Daimler-Benz Aerospace Airbus and then DaimlerChrysler in 1998, while Belgian and Turkish industry also joined the programme.

»

In 1995 is was announced that the Airbus Military Company would be established to take industrial responsibility for the FLA, but in 1997 much of the programme's government funding was withdrawn, while Germany explored the possibility of working with Ukraine's Antonov to create a variant of the An-70 to satisfy its airlift needs. By 1999, the idea of a Westernised An-70 had been dismissed, however.

Meanwhile, an international FLA request for proposals (RFP), dated from September 1997, was issued in January 1999, while an alternative Future Transport Aircraft RFP had emerged the previous July. Airbus Military delivered the A400M design proposal in February 1999 and this complex situation was resolved on July 27, 2000, when Belgium, France, Germany, Italy, Spain, Turkey and the UK announced their acceptance of the A400M proposal.

The programme's European component was agreed by the Organisation Conjointe de Coopération en matière d'Armement (OCCAR) and work proceeded under a 2003 contract. OCCAR is the contract holder on behalf of the European nations, while sales outside the organisation, to Malaysia, for example, are handled directly with Airbus Defence and Space as Airbus Military has since become.

As a complex international military aircraft programme employing a brand new, multi-national powerplant, A400M development was never going to be entirely plain sailing. Technological and industrial-

political issues affected the programme, especially as Airbus underwent a major internal restructure, pushing back delivery timelines. However, the concept was good and the partners persevered such that when the first A400M took the type's maiden flight on December 11, 2009, it ushered in a new era of airlift capability.

Subsequent software issues have been overcome, while a widely publicised but largely misunderstood fleet-wide grounding after a propeller gearbox problem was discovered in 2016 was overcome successfully in co-operation with the manufacturer.

Indeed, while unfortunate, it actually served to demonstrate just how robust the A400M engineering and support system has become, so early in the aircraft's operational lifetime.

With its combination of moderately swept wings and powerful turboprop engines, the A400M is considerably more fuel efficient at lower altitudes than the turbofan C-17, yet faster at higher altitudes than the superlative Hercules. Its capacious hold and excellent payload also place it between the C-17 and Hercules in lifting capability, yet it will ultimately offer all the rough field and tactical flexibility of the latter.

Above right: **The A400M's carefully designed undercarriage distributes the aircraft's weight on the ground, enabling remarkable runway performance for such a large aircraft. This machine, ZM400, was the first Atlas delivered to the RAF.** Paul Crouch/© UK MoD Crown Copyright 2017

Numbers XXIV and LXX Squadrons draw their A400Ms from Brize Norton's pooled fleet, with 206(R) Sqn taking additional aircraft as required for trials work. Steve Lympany/© UK MoD Crown Copyright 2017

Specification

Airbus Defence and Space A400M Atlas C.Mk 1	
Powerplant	four 11,000shp EuroProp International TP400 turboprops
Length	138ft 5½in (42.20m)
Height	48ft 2¾in (14.70m)
Wingspan	139ft 1¼in (42.40m)
Maximum speed	400kt (741km/h)
Maximum range	4,100nm (7,593km)
Maximum altitude	40,000ft
Maximum payload	81,600lb (37,000kg)

Above: **Although superficially similar in configuration to the Hercules, Atlas is a considerably larger aircraft, easily identified by its swept flying surfaces and multi-bladed propellers.** © UK MoD Crown Copyright 2017

Service Variants

Designation	First Delivery	Status
A400M Atlas C.Mk 1	November 17, 2014	Operational

Service Operators

Unit	Type	First Delivery
XXIV Sqn	A400M Atlas C.Mk 1	2014
30 Sqn	A400M Atlas C.Mk 1	Scheduled to become second frontline squadron
LXX Sqn	A400M Atlas C.Mk 1	2015 (reformed 2014)

By summer 2017, No. LXX Sqn was employing the A400M globally in its strategic capacity, while No. XXIV Sqn was delivering trained crews alongside its C-17 and Hercules output. Meanwhile, No. 206 (Reserve) Heavy Aircraft Test & Evaluation Squadron was busily extending and clearing the type's tactical capability, including natural surface runway and load-dropping trials. The RAF expects to take the last of 22 aircraft on order around 2021, with full operational capability in the tactical role declared soon after. Airbus's test crews nicknamed the A400M 'Grizzly' during the pre-delivery trials phase, but the RAF has adopted a name suggested by then Chief of the Air Staff Sir Stephen Dalton and the type is officially known as 'Atlas', while the term 'A400' is more commonly heard in use at its RAF Brize Norton base. ◉

Boeing/L-3 Communications RC-135W

The RAF's second Airseeker attended Exercise Red Flag in January 2017. Sgt Neil Bryden/© UK MoD Crown Copyright 2017

ROLE: Airseeker is a dedicated electronic surveillance aircraft that can be employed in all theatres on strategic and tactical missions. Its sensors 'soak up' electronic emissions from communications, radar and other systems.

CAPABILITY: Airseeker employs multi-discipline Weapons System Officer (WSO) and Weapons System Operator (WSOp) specialists whose mission is to survey elements of the electromagnetic spectrum in order to derive intelligence for commanders.

TYPE HISTORY: When it flew its Model 367-80 'Dash 80' prototype for the first time on July 15, 1954, Boeing hoped the aircraft

This image: **The forest of antennas serving the Airseeker's sensor suite becomes particularly obvious in silhouette.** SAC Blake Carruthers/© UK MoD Crown Copyright 2017

Inset: **Its KC-135 airframe may date from the 1960s, but Airseeker has thoroughly modern intelligence gathering capabilities.** © UK MoD Crown Copyright 2017

would take the airlines by storm. Extrapolating technology used on the B-47 and B-52 jet bombers, the aircraft represented a quantum leap directly into the jet age compared to the company's piston-engined Model 367 Stratocruiser. With its swept wing and four-jet powerplant, carried in discrete underwing nacelles, the Dash 80 was the most modern commercial transport available.

Yet the airlines were left unimpressed and it was the US Air Force, realising it needed a jet tanker to support its jet bombers, that saw the Dash 80 into production. In September 1955 it ordered its first KC-135A Stratotanker, Boeing

modifying the Dash 80 to trial a 'flying boom' refuelling system. The Stratotanker entered service on June 28, 1957 and Boeing continued development along this military line under the company designation Model 717.

The airlines had been unimpressed by the Dash 80's cabin width, which was too narrow for six-abreast seating, and Boeing therefore returned to the Dash 80 concept, widening the cabin and developing a series of successful airliners as the Model 707.

Boeing built 732 KC-135s in different variants, many of them ultimately re-engined with the modern CFM56 turbofan, known as

Airseeker
(Rivet Joint)

Specification

Boeing/L-3 Communications RC-135W Airseeker (Rivet Joint)	
Powerplant	four 21,600lb st (96kN) CFM International F108-CF-201 turbofan engines
Length	135ft (41.10m)
Height	42ft (12.80m)
Wingspan	131ft (39.90m)
Wing area	2,433sqft (226.03m²)
Maximum take-off weight	around 297,000lb (133,633kg)
Maximum airspeed	470kt (870km/h)
Range	around 3,900 miles (6,500km)
Service ceiling	39,000ft

This aircraft, ZZ664, was the first Airseeker delivered. Here it departs Waddington on May 23, 2014 for its maiden operational sortie. Sgt Si Pugsley/© UK MoD Crown Copyright 2017

the F108 in military service. These aircraft are designated KC-135R. There was also a line of C-135 transports, EC-135 command posts, RC-135 intelligence gatherers and a host of other variants, with the KC and RC remaining in widespread service.

Developed under Boeing's Model 739 series, the first of a long line of RC-135 variants was ordered in 1962. This photographic-reconnaissance RC-135A entered service during the mid-1960s, followed by the first of the electronic intelligence gatherers, the RC-135B. The precedent for modifying KC airframes to RC standard was set in 1972, with the conversion of three KC-135As as RC-135Ds for the Rivet Brass mission. All subsequent RC variants were produced by conversion/upgrade, mostly from C, KC and RC standards, culminating in the RC-135V and RC-135W, operated under the Rivet Joint codename that has become internationally,

and officially recognised in USAF parlance, as the type's name.

In June 2011, 51 Sqn flew the final BAe Nimrod R.Mk 1 sortie of its 37-year association with the type. Plans were under way for the aircraft's replacement under a project known as Airseeker, which had begun the previous March. It envisaged the acquisition of three RC-135W Rivet Joint aircraft for delivery from 2013. The machines were to be converted from USAF KC-135R airframes and L-3 Communications in Greenville, Texas was chosen to perform the work as the USAF's experienced Rivet Joint contractor. The work began in March 2011.

On November 12, 2013, No. 51 Sqn took delivery of the UK's first Rivet Joint, operating its maiden operational sortie on May 23, 2014. The second aircraft arrived in August 2015 and the third on June 8, 2017. For the purposes of sensor and system upgrades, the trio are

considered an extension of the USAF Rivet Joint fleet, ensuring they remain at the cutting edge of capability.

Rivet Joint has been deployed extensively for Operation Shader and on other operational taskings. It has been formally named Airseeker, but is almost universally known in service as Rivet Joint or simply 'RJ'. ⊙

Service Variants

Designation	First Delivery	Status
Airseeker	November 2013	Operational

Service Operators

Unit	Type	First Delivery
51 Sqn	Airseeker	November 2013

Large cheek fairings cover antenna arrays on the RJ's lower forward fuselage. Sgt Si Pugsley/© UK MoD Crown Copyright 2017

Boeing
Chinook

With its twin-rotor layout and somewhat utilitarian appearance, the Chinook is among the RAF's most distinctive aircraft. SAC Mark Parkinson/© UK MoD Crown Copyright 2017

Resilience commitment. A Chinook crew comprises two pilots and two crewmen, supplemented by specialists dependent upon mission requirements.

CAPABILITY:

In addition to its traditional war fighting roles, the Chinook's lifting capability is held at readiness under the National Resilience commitment to respond to emergencies in the UK; in recent years these have included resupplying snowbound farmers in Northern Ireland and moving tons of aggregate to help reconstruct flood defences damaged by winter storms.

The current operational Chinook fleet comprises Mk 4 and Mk 6 aircraft, fitted with digital glass cockpits. The Mk 6 also benefits from a Digital Automatic Flight Control System (DAFCS, pronounced 'daffics'), greatly enhancing handling and safety, particularly when operating in recirculating dust or snow conditions. The extended-range Mk 3, or 'fat tank' aircraft carries double the fuel load of a standard Chinook and having been upgraded to a glass cockpit configuration, returns to the fleet as the Chinook HC.Mk 5.

The Mk 4 will be further modified with the embodiment of DAFCS, resulting in the Chinook HC.Mk 6A configuration. The type »

Below: **Maritime operations off HMS _Ocean_ are a key element in the Chinook's role within Joint Helicopter Command. These aircraft were embarked along with Army Air Corp (AAC) Apaches in September 2016.** PO(Phot) Si Ethell/© UK MoD Crown Copyright 2017

ROLE:

The Chinook is an extremely capable and highly versatile support helicopter that can be operated from land or sea bases into a range of diverse environments, from the Arctic to the desert or jungle. The aircraft may be armed and is fitted with a suite of self-defence equipment allowing it to operate across the battlespace. Chinooks are primarily used for trooping, resupply and battlefield casualty evacuation (casevac).

With its triple-hook external load system, internal cargo winch, roller conveyor fit and large reserves of power, the aircraft can lift a wide variety of complex underslung or internal freight, including vehicles. It can carry up to 55 troops or up to approximately 10 tonnes of mixed cargo.

Secondary roles include search and rescue (SAR), and supporting a wide variety of specialist tasks, including the National

This Chinook HC2 was at Kandahar during Operation Herrick in 2010.
SAC Tim Laurence/© UK MoD Crown Copyright 2017

will continue to play a key role in UK Defence activity, with the Chinook Sustainment Programme aiming to build on the platform's success, recapitalising existing airframes and extending the capability out to 2040.

TYPE HISTORY:
In 1956, the US Vertol company began work on a design to satisfy a US Army medium-lift helicopter requirement. In 1958 it revealed its Model 114 proposal, which became the Boeing Model 114 when the aerospace giant took over Vertol in 1960. The US Army had ordered an initial five YCH-1B prototypes based on the

Vertol 114 in 1959 and the type achieved its first flight, under the Boeing-Vertol name, on September 21, 1961.

A service-wide reorganisation of US military aircraft designations in 1962 saw the YCH-1B, by now named Chinook, become the YCH-47A. The production CH-47A followed, for service entry on August 16, 1962. Chinook capability was more than adequately proven during the Vietnam War and a series of improved variants followed, culminating in today's extremely advanced CH-47F.

The RAF's Chinook procurement dates back to March 1967, when 15 CH-47B helicopters

were ordered to replace the Bristol Belvedere fleet. (It should be noted that the CH-47 designation has never been applied in RAF service.) That first order was cancelled in November 1967 under defence budget cuts, only to be resurrected and then cancelled again in 1971.

A 1978 order for 33 Chinook HC.Mk 1 aircraft, based on the CH-47C, was more successful and the RAF's first frontline Chinook squadron, No. 18, reformed at RAF Odiham on August 4, 1981. The following April, the Chinook was famously thrown into action after five brand-new aircraft were loaded aboard

Crews convert onto the Chinook with 28 Squadron at RAF Benson. These HC4s were involved in underslung load training in April 2016, with the more distant aircraft wearing the unit's centenary colours.
SAC Connor Payne/© UK MoD Crown Copyright 2017

Specification

Boeing Chinook HC.Mk 6	
Powerplant	two Honeywell T55-L-714A turboshaft engines, each rated at 4,168shp maximum continuous power
Length	98ft 10½in (30.14m)
Height (rotors turning)	18ft 11in (5.77m)
Rotor diameter (each)	60ft (18.29m)
Maximum cruising speed	160kt (296km/h)
Maximum density altitude	15,000ft
Payload	up to 55 troops or around 22,000lb (10,000kg) of freight
Armament	two 7.62mm M134 Miniguns and one 7.62mm M60D machine gun

MV *Atlantic Conveyor* bound for the Falkland Islands. After an Argentine Exocet missile struck the ship, only one Chinook was left operational and ZA718/BN 'Bravo November' returned exceptional service under the most difficult conditions.

Eight more HC.Mk 1s were ordered in 1983 and delivered to an upgraded standard with more powerful engines and improved cockpits equipped for night-vision goggles (NVGs). When composite units replaced the metal rotor blades on some HC1s, the aircraft were redesignated HC.Mk 1B, but a far more ambitious upgrade came with the HC.Mk 2. All 32 surviving Mk 1 airframes were scheduled for return to Boeing for modification to this latest standard, equivalent to CH-47D. Three new-build HC.Mk 2s were also ordered, along with six of the slightly modified HC.Mk 2A and eight HC.Mk 3 helicopters, loosely based on the US Army MH-47E and intended for a variety of specialist operations.

While the Mk 1 had served through the Falklands and 1991 Gulf Wars, the Mk 2 saw extensive combat over the Balkans, Iraq and Afghanistan, under Operation Herrick. During the Herrick deployment, the Chinook Force began a major change as Project Julius cycled the HC2s through a glass-cockpit programme that brought them up to HC.Mk 4 standard.

The Mk 3s, previously suffering avionics issues and restricted to UK service, emerge from Julius equipped to a similar standard and designated HC.Mk 5.

In December 2015, the RAF received the last of 14 Chinook HC.Mk 6 helicopters ordered in 2009 and based on the CH-47F. These also feature the Thales cockpit installed under Project Julius, but include more powerful engines and, crucially, the Boeing DAFCS, which revolutionises Chinook capability. Such is the improvement in performance, that the HC4 fleet will receive DAFCS in due course. •

Service Operators

Unit	Type	First Delivery
7 Sqn	Chinook HC.Mk 6	2015
18 Sqn	Chinook HC.Mk 4	2012
27 Sqn	Chinook HC.Mk 4	2012
28 Sqn	Chinook HC.Mk 4	2012

Below: **Exercise Black Alligator, held in the US, enables RAF Chinook and AAC Apache crews the opportunity to work together again in a desert environment, as they had so effectively in Afghanistan.** SAC Nicholas Egan/© UK MoD Crown Copyright 2017

Service Variants

Designation	First Delivery/Notes	Status
Chinook HC.Mk 1	December 2, 1980	Survivors upgraded to HC.Mk 2 standard
Chinook HC.Mk 1B	HC.Mk 1 with composite rotor blades	Survivors upgraded to HC.Mk 2 standard
Chinook HC.Mk 2	September 10, 1993	Survivors upgraded to HC.Mk 4 standard
Chinook HC.Mk 2A		Survivors upgraded to HC.Mk 4 standard
Chinook HC.Mk 3		Survivors upgraded to HC.Mk 5 standard
Chinook HC.Mk 4	2012	Operational
Chinook HC.Mk 5		Upgrade of HC.Mk 3 under way
Chinook HC.Mk 6	2014	Operational
Chinook HC.Mk 6A		Planned upgrade of 38 HC.Mk 4 airframes

Above: **Primary access to the Chinook's capacious cabin is via the rear loading ramp.** SAC Cathy Sharples/© UK MoD Crown Copyright 2017

Boeing C-17A
Globemaster III

ROLE: The C-17 Globemaster III is a long-range, heavy-lift strategic transport aircraft that can operate close to a potential area of operations for combat, peacekeeping or humanitarian missions worldwide.

CAPABILITY: C-17 is capable of rapid, strategic delivery of troops and all types of cargo to main operating bases anywhere in the world. The Globemaster's load-bearing rear ramp and digitally controlled loading systems, combined with the skills of its crews and ground handlers, enable large, complex items of equipment, including Chinook helicopters, military vehicles and other heavy items of specialist kit to be loaded.

It can transport 100,000lb (45,360kg) of freight more than 4,500nm (8,334km) while flying at altitudes above 35,000ft. The aircraft's design enables high-angle, steep approaches at relatively slow speeds, allowing it to operate into small, austere airfields and onto runways as short as 3,500ft long and just 90ft wide.

TYPE HISTORY: The Royal Air Force had been without an organic outsize strategic lift capability since the Short Belfast was withdrawn in 1976, relying, ironically, on civilian operated Belfasts for the movement of such loads during the 1982 Falklands War and making use of chartered freighters. By the end of the 1990s it had become clear that this capability gap ought to be filled, and in 2000 the Ministry of Defence (MoD) agreed a seven-year 'lease and support' contract with Boeing and the US Air Force (USAF) for four C-17A Globemaster III strategic transports.

On August 28, 1981, the USAF had chosen the McDonnell Douglas C-17 as winner of its C-X competition for a new military transport aircraft primarily to replace the Lockheed C-141 StarLifter. The C-17's development process was less than straightforward, however, a complex and changing procurement schedule delaying first flight until September 15, 1991. Internal manoeuvrings »

The C-17's rear ramp facilitates loading, but also becomes a load-bearing extension of the cabin floor when closed.
SAC Cathy Sharples/© UK MoD Crown Copyright 2017

Service Variants

Designation	First Delivery	Status
C-17A Globemaster III	May 2001	Operational

Service Operators

Unit	Type	First Delivery
99 Sqn	C-17A Globemaster III	May 2001

at McDonnell Douglas further complicated the programme as C-17 responsibility moved between divisions and although the 1993 first delivery to an operational USAF unit was from the original manufacturer, in 1997 the C-17 became a Boeing product on the latter's acquisition of its rival.

The C-17A had become the Globemaster III on February 5, 1993, following on from the USAF's Douglas C-74 Globemaster and C-124 Globemaster II post-war piston-engined transports. By the time the UK defined its initial C-17 requirement the type was well established in service and the RAF benefitted from access to the global C-17 support network and supply chain. In UK service, the type is typically referred to as C-17 or Globemaster, no formal RAF role/numerical designation (Globemaster C.Mk 1 would have followed the regular pattern of aircraft titles) being applied, since the aircraft was initially leased.

Number 99 Squadron reformed at RAF Brize Norton to operate the aircraft, which rapidly became a stalwart and key enabler of the airbridge operation that sustained UK operations in Afghanistan. Even at the peak of Operation Herrick, however, the C-17 serviced humanitarian and operational commitments elsewhere and rather than taking an option to extend the C-17 lease by two years, the MoD bought the initial four aircraft and ordered a fifth in 2006.

Continued demand saw a sixth ordered in 2007, a seventh in 2009 and the eighth and, to date, final example in 2012. The latter was ordered and delivered within weeks at a reported cost of £200 million according to an MoD press statement.

With the end of Herrick, 99 Sqn has continued flying many of the types of mission in which the C-17 excelled during the operation, moving personnel and equipment, and performing aeromedical evacuation

Specification

Boeing C-17A Globemaster III	
Powerplant	four 40,400lb st (179.90kN) Pratt & Whitney F117-PW-100 turbofans
Length overall	174ft (53.04m)
Height overall	55ft 1in (16.79m)
Wingspan	169ft 9in (51.74m)
Wing area	3,800sqft (353.03m²)
Maximum take-off weight	585,000lb (265,350kg)
Cruising speed at 28,000ft	450kt (833km/h)
Range with 100,000lb (45,360kg) payload	more than 4,500nm (8,334km)
Service ceiling	45,000ft
Maximum payload (2.5g load factor)	169,000lb (76,655kg)

Main image: **Globemaster ZZ176 received special tail markings for 99Sqn's 99th anniversary. The C-17's winglets improve its aerodynamic efficiency in cruising flight, while engine exhaust gases blowing over the extended wing flaps improve its field performance.** Steve Lympany/© UK MoD Crown Copyright 2017

Incorporating a typical early-2000s glass cockpit, the C-17 also provides each of its crew with a head-up display. SAC Cathy Sharples/© UK MoD Crown Copyright 2017

missions with a suite of surgical facilities and staff on board. Support to deployed operations remains as important as ever and RAF C-17s are regular visitors to allied forward bases, particularly in connection with French anti-terrorist work in Africa.

Humanitarian flights, typically planned and flown wherever needed at very short notice, are common 99 Sqn trade, while the fact remains that when a C-17 taxies onto an airfield ramp anywhere in the world, with the Union Jack painted large on its side, there can be no doubt that UK interests are involved. ☉

'Royal Air Force' titles and the Union Jack proudly proclaim ZZ174's ownership. This aircraft was the last of those acquired under the original seven-year lease. SAC Cathy Sharples/© UK MoD Crown Copyright 2017

A Weapons Systems Operator (Crewman) lends scale to the C-17's vast cargo hold. SAC Cathy Sharples/© UK MoD Crown Copyright 2017

Lockheed Martin C-130J
Hercules

ROLE: The Hercules is the RAF's primary tactical transport aircraft and in its current C.Mk 4 and C.Mk 5 versions of the C-130J-30 and C-130J, respectively, has been the backbone of UK operational tactical mobility tasks since it was brought into service in 1999. It is frequently employed to operate into countries or regions where there is a threat to aircraft; its performance, tactics and defensive systems make it the ideal platform for such tasks.

CAPABILITY: The aircraft is highly flexible, with the ability to airdrop a variety of stores and paratroopers, and operate from natural surface landing zones. To conduct these missions it is vital that Hercules crews are highly skilled in low-level flying. The aircraft performs in the same roles at night using night-vision goggles (NVGs), while station keeping equipment (SKE) enables it to remain in formation during poor weather. Long-range capabilities are enhanced with air-to-air refuelling, while the Air Survival Rescue Apparatus may be mounted in the cabin for search and rescue missions, enabling the Hercules to airdrop life rafts and emergency supplies.

TYPE HISTORY: On February 2, 1951, the USAF issued a General Operational Requirement for an aircraft to replace its large fleets of Curtiss C-46, and Fairchild C-82 and C-119 piston-engined transports. Lockheed responded with its L-206 design, which the USAF chose as the winning contender on July 2, 1951, ordering two YC-130A prototypes based on the proposal.

The first production C-130A Hercules entered service in December 1956 and Lockheed went on to create a bewildering array of variants and subvariants for the US and foreign militaries, and civilian market. After the Armstrong Whitworth AW681 vertical take-off transport had been abandoned on the

Above: **The C.Mk 4 is the longer of the two second-generation Hercules variants in RAF service.** Sqn Ldr Andy Wasley/© UK MoD Crown Copyright 2017

Underwing fuel tanks are available for sorties when long range or extended endurance is particularly important, as demonstrated by this C4. Note also the six-bladed propellers, compared to the four-bladed units of the C-130K. SAC Cathy Sharples/© UK MoD Crown Copyright 2017

Specification

Lockheed Martin C-130J Hercules	
Powerplant	four 4,700shp Rolls-Royce AE2100D3 turboprops
Length, C.Mk 4	112ft 9in (34.34m)
Length, C.Mk 5	97ft 9in (29.77m)
Height	38ft 4¾in (11.70m)
Wingspan	132ft 7in (40.38m)
Wing area	1,745sqft (162.12m²)
Cruising speed	320kt (593km/h)
Ferry range, C.Mk 4	2,650nm (4,908km)
Ferry range, C.Mk 5	2,850nm (5,078km)
Maximum altitude	40,000ft
Cruising altitude	28,000ft

drawing board, the RAF found itself needing to replace its piston-engined Blackburn Beverley and Handley Page Hastings transports, while augmenting the Armstrong Whitworth Argosy turboprop. Sixty-six Hercules were therefore ordered, essentially to C-130H standard, but designated C-130K for export to the UK.

Known to the RAF as Hercules C.Mk 1 (the C-130K designation only came into regular use as a differentiator after the C-130J entered service), the first aircraft completed its maiden

Above: **RAF Hercules range globally on humanitarian work. This example was at Kathmandu, Nepal in May 2015, after an earthquake struck the country.** Sgt Neil Bryden/© UK MoD Crown Copyright 2017

flight on October 19, 1966. The type entered service in 1967, but defence cuts in 1975 saw 13 Hercules aircraft withdrawn and two squadrons disbanded.

Even in this reduced state, the Hercules fleet was crucial to UK operations, a fact emphasised by the 1982 Falklands War. It very quickly became apparent that the Hercules would be required to mount non-stop return sorties to the Falklands from Ascension Island and a crash programme of inflight-refuelling probe »

Service Variants

Designation	First Delivery	Status
Hercules C.Mk 1	April 1967	Sixty-six aircraft known as C-130K to Lockheed, withdrawn
Hercules C.Mk 1P		Twenty-five C.Mk 1s equipped with inflight-refuelling probes, withdrawn
Hercules C.Mk 1K		Six C.Mk 1s equipped with inflight-refuelling probes and rear-fuselage hose drum units as air-refuelling tankers, withdrawn
Hercules W.Mk 2		One C.Mk 1 modified for meteorological research, withdrawn
Hercules C.Mk 3		Thirty C.Mk 1s modified with a 15ft (4.57m) fuselage stretch for increased capacity, withdrawn
Hercules C.Mk 3P		Twenty-nine C.Mk 3s modified with inflight-refuelling probes, withdrawn
Hercules C.Mk 4	Nov 21, 1999	Fifteen aircraft known as C-130J-30 to Lockheed Martin, operational
Hercules C.Mk 5	1999	Ten aircraft known as C-130J to Lockheed Martin, operational

installation began. Modified aircraft were designated C.Mk 1P; the first refuelling contact occurred on May 3, 1982, with a Handley Page Victor tanker, and the first combat mission on the 16th.

With the VC10 tanker conversion programme yet to gather pace and the heavy Victor commitment in the South Atlantic, the versatile Hercules was also selected for conversion as a tanker, six aircraft receiving hose drum units (HDUs) and refuelling probes. The first completed its maiden and delivery flights on July 5, 1982. In the conflict's immediate aftermath, the C.Mk 1K took a vital role supporting RAF BAe Harriers and, subsequently, McDonnell Douglas Phantoms providing Falkland Islands air defence.

Meanwhile, in 1978 a conversion programme had begun to produce 30 Hercules C.Mk 3 aircraft by stretching the fuselage of the C1 to achieve a dramatic increase in cabin capacity. Lockheed produced the initial C3, flying it for the first time on December 3, 1979, but Marshall produced the remainder. Indeed, the Cambridge-based company has been instrumental in the Hercules programme since its inception, the first RAF Hercules having

been delivered direct to Marshall, which subsequently performed all the major fleet conversion work and continues to support the C-130J. Later, 29 C3s received inflight-refuelling probes to become C.Mk 3P aircraft.

A December 1993 MoD requirement identified the need for a Hercules replacement and although the European FLA was considered, the only substitute for a Hercules turned out to be a Hercules, in the shape of the more powerful Lockheed C-130J, a next-generation machine then under development and featuring the latest avionics systems.

The December 1994 order comprised ten standard C-130J aircraft and 15 of the longer C-130J-30, with first delivery (of a J-30) in August 1998. The initial operational example reached RAF Lyneham, then the RAF's Hercules base, on November 21, 1999.

Designated Hercules C.Mk 4 in service, the C-130J-30 is just a little shorter than the C3, while the Hercules C.Mk 5 has the same fuselage length as the C1. Inflight-refuelling probes are installed as standard, while the type's improved range enables most sorties to be flown without the characteristic underwing fuel tanks of the legacy versions.

Service Operators

Unit	Type	First Delivery
XXIV Sqn	Hercules	2002
47 Sqn	Hercules	

Having worked intensively during Operations Telic and Herrick alongside the legacy Hercules fleet, the C-130J has accumulated flying hours rather more rapidly than had been projected. It was identified in the 2010 Strategic Defence and Security Review for withdrawal from service in 2022, a decade earlier than originally planned, while the C-130K was retired on October 28, 2013 after almost five decades on the frontline.

By now the A400M programme was well advanced. The Atlas was always earmarked to replace the Hercules and although its tactical capability is likely to have expanded dramatically by 2022, the C-130J clearly had an important tactical role to play until the A400M was fully established. The 2015 Strategic Defence and Security Review reflected this thinking, with the announcement that 14 Hercules C4s will remain in service until 2030, with funding allocated not only for their operations, but also for upgrading and life extension. ⊚

Hercules C5 ZH880 was painted for 47 Sqn's centenary in 2016. It serves to illustrate the variant's length compared to the C4, being shorter both fore and aft of the wing. Paul Crouch/© UK MoD Crown Copyright 2017

A Hercules seen from a Voyager tanker on exercise over the North Sea. This aircraft combination is particularly important on the Falkland Islands, where a single Hercules is primarily tasked with search and rescue, and maritime patrol, relying on the Voyager for extended mission endurance.
LAC Hanna/© UK MoD Crown Copyright 2017

ZH106 was the penultimate RAF Sentry. The type is based on the classic Boeing 707, the final E-3D, ZH107, accounting for the last 707 airframe off the line. © UK MoD Crown Copyright 2017

Boeing

E-3D Sentry AEW.Mk 1

ROLE: Commonly known as AWACS (Airborne Warning And Control System) after its US nomenclature, the E-3D Sentry AEW.Mk 1 is an airborne early warning (AEW) and command and control aircraft.

CAPABILITY: The Sentry monitors airspace to provide threat detection of adversary aircraft and situational awareness on friendly assets. Information gathered by the Northrop Grumman APY-2 radar is processed by the mission crew and disseminated via a variety of data links and communication systems.

Sentry also has the capability to detect ships, relaying information to maritime aircraft or allied vessels for further investigation. Its electronic support measures equipment enables the E-3D to gather emissions from other radar systems and emitters, enhancing the crew's

Specification

Boeing E-3D Sentry AEW.Mk 1	
Powerplant	four 24,000lb st (107kN) CFM International CFM56-2A3 turbofans
Length	152ft 11in (46.61m)
Height	41ft 4in (12.60m)
Wingspan	145ft 9in (44.42m)
Wing area	3,050sqft (83.40m²)
Empty weight	185,000lb (83,990kg)
Maximum take-off weight	334,000lb (151,636kg)
Cruising speed	Mach 0.72
Rate of climb	2,000ft/min (610m/min)
Range	5,000nm (8,046km)
Endurance	10 hours
Service ceiling	43,000ft (13,106m)

understanding of the environment in which it is operating.

TYPE HISTORY: Seeking a modern, jet-powered replacement for the piston-engined types it was operating in the AEW role, on July 23, 1970, the US Air Force chose the Boeing 707-320 airliner as the base airframe for a new Airborne Warning And Control System aircraft.

Modified with a Westinghouse AN/APY-1 radar system, its antenna covered by a massive rotating radome held over the rear fuselage, the first of two EC-137D prototypes completed its initial flight on February 5, 1972. After an extensive test programme, the E-3A production version entered service in March 1977. Although the type is officially named 'Sentry', the USAF designates it E-3 AWACS.

In January 1972, just days before the EC-137D took off for the first time, 8 Sqn, RAF, re-formed to operate the Avro Shackleton

This Sentry was forward deployed for Operation Telic, over Iraq, in 2003. Staff Sgt Matthew Hannen (USAF)/© UK MoD Crown Copyright 2017

Operation Shader is among the E-3D's most important commitments. This aircraft was arriving in-theatre in January 2015. © UK MoD Crown Copyright 2017

The E-3D is unusual in having a refuelling receptacle in its upper forward fuselage compatible with boom-equipped tankers, and a probe for use with hose-and-drogue tankers, including **Voyager.** SAC Andy Stevens/© UK MoD Crown Copyright 2017

Service Variants

Designation	First Delivery	Status
E-3D Sentry AEW.Mk 1	March 26, 1991	Operational

Service Operators

Unit	Type	First Delivery
8 Sqn	E-3D Sentry AEW.Mk 1	July 1991

AEW.Mk 2, a conversion of the Shackleton MR.Mk 2 to accommodate radar systems recently removed from Fleet Air Arm Fairey Gannet AEW platforms. With its dedicated and highly skilled crews, the Shackleton provided a useful stopgap capability and it was expected that the Nimrod AEW.Mk 3 would replace it sometime in the early to mid-1980s.

A dramatic modification of the Nimrod MR.Mk 1, the AEW.Mk 3 first flew on July 16, 1980, but suffered insurmountable technical problems, primarily caused by the incompatibility of its avionics and airframe; it was finally cancelled early in 1987.

The large rotodome, strut-mounted over its rear fuselage, dominates the Sentry's appearance. It slowly rotates even when the radar is not in use, helping keep the system's bearings lubricated. SAC Andy Stevens/© UK MoD Crown Copyright 2017

With an urgent need to replace the piston-engined Shackleton, the Ministry of Defence looked to a solution that had previously been suggested during the Nimrod AEW.Mk 3 programme and ordered seven E-3s.

Officially designated Sentry AEW.Mk 1 in RAF service, but commonly known as E-3D, the new aircraft differed from the US fleet in its powerplant of more efficient CFM56 engines. The Shackleton remained on strength until 1991, 8 Sqn taking its first E-3D at RAF Waddington, Lincolnshire in July. Little more than a year later, the type was in action over the Balkans, before making a valuable

contribution to Operation Warden over northern Iraq in 1994.

Today the Sentry is fully integrated into the ISTAR Force, yet retains its core competencies of airborne early warning and airspace management. Its capability is no more appreciated than in the skies over Iraq and Syria, where an ongoing commitment to Operation Shader sees the E-3D deconflicting airspace, providing 'big picture' situational awareness for Coalition aircraft and early warning of aircraft movements outside Coalition control. The 2015 Strategic Defence and Security Review called for Sentry to remain in service until 2035. ⊙

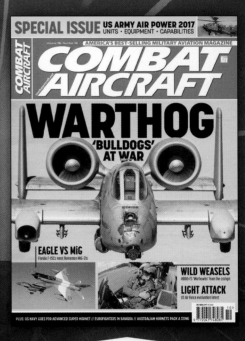

Lockheed Martin F-35B Lightning

Left: **A single British F-35B, accompanied by a pair of US Marine Corps jets, visited the UK in summer 2016.** SAC Tim Laurence/© UK MoD Crown Copyright 2017

Above right: **Windows above and below the forward fuselage serve the F-35B's sensors. It is equipped for probe-and-drogue refuelling.** SAC Tim Laurence/© UK MoD Crown Copyright 2017

ROLE: The F-35B Lightning fifth-generation combat aircraft will operate alongside the Typhoon. Lightning is a multi-role machine capable of conducting missions including air-to-surface, electronic warfare, intelligence gathering and air-to-air simultaneously.

CAPABILITY: The aircraft combines advanced sensors and mission systems with low-observable technology, or 'stealth', which enables it to operate undetected in hostile airspace. Its integrated sensors, sensor fusion and data linking provide the pilot with unprecedented situational awareness. The pilot is able to share information gathered by the jet with other platforms using secure data links, and/or use the information to employ weapons or electronic means. The F-35B's short take-off and vertical landing (STOVL) capability allows it to operate from the new 'Queen Elizabeth'-class aircraft carriers and the vessels of allied nations, as well as short airstrips.

TYPE HISTORY: Lockheed Martin's F-35 Lightning II embodies capabilities based on thinking developed through evolving requirements since at least 1983, when the US Navy launched its Advanced Tactical Aircraft (ATA) programme to find a stealthy replacement for the Grumman A-6 Intruder. That same year, the Defense Advanced Research Projects Agency (DARPA) began its Advanced Short Take-Off/Vertical Landing (ASTOVL) effort, looking to develop a supersonic successor to the Harrier.

Pulling *g* as he manoeuvres for the camera, Squadron Leader Hugh Nicols drags 'streamers' out of the damp Atlantic air on the 2016 flight to the UK. SAC Tim Laurence/© UK MoD Crown Copyright 2017

Two classified programmes ran under ASTOVL, which was always intended to produce information of value to the US and UK. The STOVL Strike Fighter (SSF) research ran from 1987 to 1994 and examined the feasibility of creating the technologies necessary for a stealthy, supersonic STOVL fighter, while the Common Affordable Lightweight Fighter (CALF) programme ran for just a year from 1993, combining the ASTOVL and SSF work into a single effort to provide a Harrier replacement specifically for the US and UK.

Meanwhile, ATA had suffered insurmountable technological and financial challenges and closed down in 1991. In 1990, however, the US Navy had already turned its attention to replacing the Grumman F-14 Tomcat, for which requirement the USAF's Advanced Tactical Fighter (ATF) was seen as a potential basis. The proposal was examined as the Naval ATF, but dismissed in 1991 as too expensive – ATF ultimately evolved into today's Lockheed Martin F-22 Raptor.

The USAF had begun a replacement programme of its own in 1990; the Multi-Role Fighter (MRF) was to succeed the General Dynamics F-16 Fighting Falcon. By 1992, MRF was also being considered as a replacement for the USAF's Fairchild Republic A-10A Thunderbolt II and US Navy McDonnell Douglas F/A-18C/D Hornet fleets. But as budgets and forces were cut following the end of the Cold War, F-16 upgrades became more attractive and with its focus on ATF, the USAF ended MRF in 1993.

More or less simultaneously and prior to the termination of NATF, the US Navy returned to the quandary of how to replace the A-6, examining new options under the Advanced-Attack/Advanced/Fighter-Attack (A-X/A/F-A) programme from 1991. Because it promised to create an aircraft of superior performance and

capability, the USAF identified A-X/A/F-A as a potential replacement for its General Dynamics F-111, McDonnell Douglas F-15E Strike Eagle and Lockheed F-117A Nighthawk platforms.

With NATF cancelled, A-X/A/F-A gained new air-to-air requirements and became the Advanced Attack/Fighter (A/F-X) and although progress was made, Congress became concerned at the number of projects under way with hopes of reaching the same or similar goals. As a result, A/F-X, ASTOVL and is components were merged under the Joint Advanced Strike Technology (JAST) programme in 1994.

JAST aimed to gather and coalesce all the formative technologies existing under the various programmes, but lasted barely a year, becoming Joint Strike Fighter (JSF) when it reached its concept definition phase in 1996. Late that year, Boeing and Lockheed Martin were awarded contracts to produce two JSF demonstrators each for a competitive fly-off, with Boeing's aircraft designated X-32 and Lockheed Martin's X-35.

In 1997, Lockheed Martin added Northrop Grumman and British Aerospace to its team, and the UK has since remained the primary overseas partner on the programme. The intention with JSF was to create a stealthy tactical aircraft in three major variants: the conventional take-off and landing (CTOL) A-model was primarily an F-16 replacement, the STOVL 'B' was intended to succeed the Harrier, and the carrierborne (CV) 'C' would belatedly fill the hole left by the US Navy's A-6, while also replacing some US Navy and Marine Corps F/A-18C/D aircraft.

Boeing was first into the air, with the X-32A, on September 18, 2000. The X-32B followed on March 29, 2001 and the test programme concluded on July 28. Lockheed Martin trailed by only a few weeks, flying the X-35A on October 24, 2000. With 'A' testing completed

Specification

Lockheed Martin F-35B Lightning	
Powerplant	one Pratt & Whitney F135 turbofan rated at 40,000lb st (177.88kN) with afterburning and 40,500lb st (180.10kN) for vertical take-off
Length	51ft 2¼in (15.60m)
Height	14ft 3½in (4.36m)
Wingspan	35ft (10.70m)
Wing area	460sqft (42.70m²)
Maximum take-off weight	around 60,000lb (27,216kg)
Maximum speed	Mach 1.6
Combat radius on internal fuel	more than 450nm (833km)
Maximum altitude	50,000ft
Armament	typically two AAMs and two bombs carried internally, with optional 25mm gun pod and underwing pylons enabling stores carriage up to 15,000lb (6,800kg)

Service Operators

Unit	Type	First Delivery
17(R) Sqn	F-35B Lightning	2014
207 Sqn	F-35B Lightning	2019
617 Sqn	F-35B Lightning	2018
809 NAS	F-35B Lightning	2023

The 2016 visit gave RAF Marham a fleeting opportunity to familiarise itself with the Lightning in a series of flypasts. Here the RAF jet and one of the USMC machines formate with a Tornado GR4, the type Lightning will replace at the Norfolk station. Cpl Ashley Keates/© UK MoD Crown Copyright 2017

on November 22, the aircraft was modified to X-35B configuration, first flying in its new form on June 23, 2001.

While Boeing had completed CV testing with the X-32A, Lockheed Martin chose to fly a dedicated X-35C, which flew for the first time on December 16, 2000. The X-35 test programme concluded on August 6, 2001.

On October 26, the Lockheed Martin/Northrop Grumman/BAE Systems team was announced as winning the JSF contract and the X-35 began to evolve into the F-35 Lightning II.

The UK formally announced its intention to acquire the F-35B in 2006. For many years, the country's JSF programme was known as Joint Combat Aircraft (JCA), which remained F-35B based until the 2010 Strategic Defence and Security Review, which switched the British requirement to the F-35C. But with the 'Queen Elizabeth'-class carrier design well advanced for STOVL, rather than the catapult and arrestor

('cat and trap') gear required for CV operations, JCA resorted back to the F-35B, at the same time increasingly becoming known as 'JSF' by programme insiders.

Squadron Leader Steve Long became the first British pilot to fly F-35, on January 26, 2010 and in July 2012 the government announced its decision to purchase an initial batch of 48 aircraft. The first of these was delivered on July 19 for trials work, a task 17 (Reserve) Squadron assumed in 2014.

The 2015 Strategic Defence and Security Review confirmed the UK's intention to buy 138 F-35Bs and subsequent work has seen a massive infrastructure upgrade begin at what will be the type's RAF/Royal Navy main operating base, RAF Marham. In British service the aircraft will be known only as Lightning, losing its 'II' (it will actually be the RAF's third Lightning, after the Lockheed P-38 and English Electric Lightning). The first frontline Lightning unit,

617 Sqn 'Dambusters' is expected to arrive at RAF Marham in spring/summer 2018 and continue working towards achieving initial operating capability (IOC) in December.

The Lightning OCU, No. 207 Sqn, will stand up at Marham on July 1, 2019, followed by a second operational unit, 809 Naval Air Squadron (NAS), in 2023. Trials aboard HMS *Queen Elizabeth* should also commence in 2018, building towards full carrier strike capability in 2020. The last of the initial 48 Lightnings is expected for delivery in January 2025, by which time a schedule for the remaining 90 aircraft, and the formation of further squadrons, will no doubt be in place. ⊘

Service Variants

Designation	First Delivery	Status
F-35B Lightning	2012	Operational test

The Harrier relied on vectored exhaust nozzles directing its jet efflux downwards for hovering and vertical take-off. The F-35B's solution is very different, with the articulated rear nozzle moving downwards to provide a major element of lift in combination with a forward-mounted, shaft-driven Rolls-Royce lift fan. SAC Tim Laurence/© UK MoD Crown Copyright 2017

Leonardo AW109SP
GrandNew

ROLE: The Leonardo AW109SP GrandNew helicopter is operated by No. 32 (The Royal) Squadron as a complement to the BAe 146 in the Command Support Air Transport role. It can be flown by a single pilot in all weather conditions, by day or night, providing site-to-site transportation for senior military commanders and government ministers in the UK and Europe. Its ability to operate into heliports or even locations with no landing facilities at all, provides the ultimate in CSAT availability and flexibility.

CAPABILITY: With its four-axis digital duplex autopilot and advanced avionics suite, the GrandNew provides its pilots with enhanced situational awareness and flight management capabilities compared to the A109E that it replaced, increasing safety and overall efficiency.

It achieves its maximum endurance of two hours 40 minutes with up to six passengers on board, while its twin-engined powerplant expands pilots' options when planning routes over built-up areas, as well as offering wide safety margins for flying in and out of confined landing sites.

TYPE HISTORY: Italy's Agusta first flew an A109 prototype on August 4, 1971 and delivered the A109A first production version of the light utility machine from 1976. Deliveries of the upgraded A109A Mk II began in September 1981, with the ultimate civilian version of the early series emerging as the A109C in 1989.

Meanwhile, the type had also found considerable favour with military operators, continuous development resulting in the A109K, equipped for military and para-military operations, including mountain rescue.

The civilian and military developments merged into a single basic airframe in the A109 Power, launched in 1993. Known as the A109E Power, the basic civilian model in the new range became available in 1996.

On April 1, 2006, AgustaWestland, formed through the merger of Agusta and the UK's Westland in 2000, was granted a contract to provide three A109E helicopters to replace a similar number of Squirrels in 32(TR) Sqn service. The Power served for a decade, although the fleet was reduced to two and then just one aircraft before its withdrawal in favour of the AW109SP GrandNew.

The GrandNew represents the latest line of A109 development under the AgustaWestland name. It is now supplied by Leonardo, since the AgustaWestland company was absorbed into a single entity by its Finmeccanica owner in April 2016, the latter simultaneously changing its name to Leonardo. ⊙

Service Operators

Unit	Type	First Delivery
32(TR) Sqn	AW109SP GrandNew	February 11, 2016

Service Variants

Designation	First Delivery	Status
A109E Power	2006	Withdrawn
AW109SP GrandNew	February 11, 2016	Operational

With its high-speed cruise and wide choice of landing sites, the AW109SP enables commanders to make multiple stops between units, or exercises, in one day, rather than potentially spending hours on the road over several days.
Cpl Ben Tritta/© UK MoD Crown Copyright 2017

Specification

Leonardo AW109SP GrandNew	
Powerplant	two Pratt & Whitney Canada PW207C turboshafts each rated at 572shp maximum continuous power
Length overall	42ft 6in (12.96m)
Height overall	11ft 2in (3.39m)
Main rotor diameter	35ft 6in (10.83m)
Maximum take-off weight	7,000lb (3,175kg)
Maximum cruising speed	156kt (289km/h)
Maximum range	464nm (859km)
Hovering ceiling out of ground effect	10,000ft
Accommodation	up to six passengers

A 60(R) Sqn Griffin HT1 in 2012. Sgt Jack Pritchard/© UK MoD Crown Copyright 2017

Bell Griffin

Specification

Bell Griffin	
Powerplant	one 1,800shp Pratt & Whitney Canada PT6T-3D Turbo Twin-Pac turboshaft
Length overall, rotors turning	56ft 1¾in (17.11m)
Height	11ft 5in (3.48m)
Main rotor diameter	46ft (14.02m)
Main rotor disc area	1,661.90sqft (154.40m²)
Maximum take-off weight	around 11,900lb (5,397kg)
Never exceed speed	140kt (259km/h)
Range with maximum payload	around 375nm (695km)
Maximum altitude	20,000ft

ROLE: Two distinct Griffin variants are in RAF service, the HAR.Mk 2, operated by 84 Squadron as a multi-role helicopter from its RAF Akrotiri base, and the HT.Mk 1, flown by 60(R) and 202(R) Sqns as part of the Defence Helicopter Flying School (DHFS). In the support helicopter role, the Griffin HAR2 carries six fully-equipped troops, or up to eight if operationally essential. It also employs underslung Bambi Buckets for fire fighting and has a vital search and rescue (SAR) mission, as well as taking force protection, military aid to civilian authorities and ISTAR roles.

CAPABILITY: The Griffin HAR2 is equipped with night-vision goggles and a FLIR/TV turret, which affords its crews a relevant night capability. Owing to the hot, arid climate of its Cyprus base, the HAR2 regularly employs its crucial fire fighting capability across the region. Other capabilities include search and rescue.

The HT1 lacks the weather radar and one or two other of the HAR2's operational features, but is equipped to deliver comprehensive multi-engine helicopter training to future frontline pilots and rear crew. It also equips 202(R) Sqn, formerly the SAR Training Unit, providing UK military helicopter pilots with SAR and mountain flying training.

TYPE HISTORY: In 1955, the US Army chose Bell's Model 204 to satisfy its requirement for a casevac and utility transport helicopter.

Service Variants

Designation	First Delivery	Status
Griffin HT.Mk 1	1997	Operational
Griffin HAR.Mk 2	April 1, 2003	Operational

The first of three XH-40 prototypes of the Model 204 completed its maiden flight on October 23, 1956. Six YH-40 development aircraft followed before the first of the HU-1A production aircraft, which quickly gained the nickname 'Huey'.

HU-1 became UH-1 under the 1962 consolidation of US military aircraft designation systems and a plethora of improved models followed, especially in response to the demands of the war in Vietnam. The Model 205 introduced a longer fuselage from 1963, initially as the UH-1D, and

the model became the basis of the Model 212, delivered to the USAF from 1970 as the UH-1N.

The Model 212 featured the unusual PT6T, a combination of two turbines driving a single shaft, for much increased power reserves. With the revised powerplant there was clearly more performance to be extracted from the airframe and Bell achieved this by installing an uprated engine and four-bladed main rotor to create the Bell 412, which first flew in 1979. The type was delivered from 1981, and in 1992 the Canadian Armed Forces ordered 100 of the CH-146 Griffon variant. Variations of the name stuck with the type, which remains in production for the civilian and para-military markets.

In RAF service, 84 Squadron operates three aircraft supplied and maintained by civilian company Cobham, but operated by experienced military aircrew. The DHFS Griffins are scheduled to be withdrawn from 2018, when the Airbus Helicopters H145 begins replacing them. ●

Service Operators

Unit	Type	First Delivery
60(R) Sqn	Griffin HT.Mk 1	1997
84 Sqn	Griffin HAR.Mk 2	2003
202(R) Sqn	Griffin HT.Mk 1	1997

Number 84 Sqn's SAR tasking is of particular importance to RAF Akrotiri. Cpl Andy Benson/© UK MoD Crown Copyright 2017

BAE Systems
Hawk

ROLE: The Hawk is operational in two very distinct variants, the Hawk T.Mk 1 (and very similar Mk 1A) and T.Mk 2. The latter has replaced the Mk 1/1A in the flying training role, bringing personnel up to fast jet operational conversion unit (OCU) input standards after they graduate from the turboprop Tucano.

The aircraft's glass cockpit and comprehensive avionics suite provide a realistic advanced fast jet training platform which, as part of the UK Military Flying Training System (UK MFTS), meets current and future standards. It allows trainees to be immersed in more complex tactical environments, 'downloading' training from the OCUs onto the Hawk, which is far more economical to fly than Tornado or Typhoon.

Previously the RAF's premier fast jet trainer, the Hawk T1 now continues in service with the Royal Air Force Aerobatic Team (RAFAT) The Red Arrows and 100 Sqn. With the former it provides an exceptional mount for formation aerobatics and with the latter it provides all manner of target facilities and threat simulation, as well as working closely in Joint Tactical Air Controller (JTAC) training.

CAPABILITY: The Mk 2's avionics enable simulations of many of the functions of a modern fighter, combined with an extensive mission debrief system that extracts maximum

This image: **The British public is perhaps most familiar with the Hawk as the mount of the Red Arrows.** SAC Ed Wright/© UK MoD Crown Copyright 2017

Below: **The angular nose profile and fin leading edge radar-warning receiver are instant Hawk T.Mk 2 recognition features.** Cpl Mark Dixon/© UK MoD Crown Copyright 2017

Service Operators

Unit	Type	Operational
IV(R) Sqn	Hawk T.Mk 2	November 24, 2011
100 Sqn	Hawk T.Mk 1/1A	September 1991
RAFAT	Hawk T.Mk 1/1A	1979

Combining the Hawk's agility and high performance with clever tactics, 100 Sqn extracts maximum training benefit out of the Mk 1 airframe. © UK MoD Crown Copyright 2017

output from every sortie. Via the aircraft's data link, for example, synthetic radar returns are generated for intercept and basic fighter manoeuvres training, yet no radar is fitted. The on board simulation capability also enables air-to-ground 'weapon drops', realistic electronic warfare (EW) training against surface-to-air missile (SAM) systems and other complex operational scenarios.

In RAFAT service the Hawk T1 is modified with a smoke generation system, while minor changes to the engine controls enable a

more immediate throttle response to that of the standard aircraft. In 100 Sqn service the T.Mk 1/1A remains largely unchanged to its previous training incarnation, the expertise of its crews lending it unique capabilities in the adversary, target facilities and JTAC training roles.

TYPE HISTORY: In 1962, the Folland

Gnat entered service to replace the de Havilland Vampire as the RAF's advanced jet trainer. An aircraft of exceptional performance, the Gnat was earmarked for eventual replacement by

the SEPECAT Jaguar B, a training variant of the famous attack aircraft. Even as the 'Jag' option began to look too expensive, however, Hawker Siddeley was working on its P.1182 trainer design as a private venture.

In 1970 the MoD acknowledged that Jaguar B was not viable and instead looked to a requirement issued in October 1968 for a jet to replace the Hunting Jet Provost T.Mk 5 basic trainer, modifying it slightly to describe an advanced trainer design. The P.1182 was chosen in October 1971, becoming the HS.1182

The Hawk T2 fleet is based entirely at RAF Valley, close to the sea and extensive low-level flying areas. © UK MoD Crown Copyright 2017

Specification

BAE Systems Hawk T.Mk 2	
Powerplant	one 6,500lb st (28.91kN) Rolls-Royce/Turbomeca Adour Mk 951 turbofan
Length	40ft 9in (12.43m)
Height	13ft 1in (3.98m)
Wingspan	32ft 7in (9.94m)
Wing area	179.64sqft (16.70m²)
Maximum take-off weight	20,000lb (9,100kg)

and then the Hawk. The Jaguar foray had not been entirely wasted, since a non-afterburning version of its Adour turbofan was selected as the Hawk powerplant. Combined with a simple, yet elegant airframe, it made for a high-performance aeroplane and a trainer of exceptional qualities.

Airborne for the first time on August 21, 1974, the Hawk required little adjustment before it was ready for service, initially with 4 Flying Training School (FTS) at RAF Valley in November 1976. By 1978 it had replaced the Gnat trainers and the following year RAFAT relinquished its own Gnats in favour of Hawks, which it debuted in 1980.

With the Cold War showing little sign of thawing, in the late 1970s the government looked to improve UK air defence. Part of the requirement called for a local air defence fighter capable of taking on enemy aircraft that had evaded the Lightning and Phantom fighter screen, and defensive SAMs.

The Hawk offered an ideal basis for such a fighter and between 1983 and 1989, some 89 aircraft were modified to T.Mk 1A standard, equipped to launch pairs of AIM-9L Sidewinder IR-guided air-to-air missiles, in addition to the centreline 30mm ADEN gun pod.

The aircraft remained in regular training and RAFAT service, their instructors and the 'Reds' remaining current in fighter tactics and exercising, latterly with the Tornado F.Mk 3, regularly. This so-called 'mixed force' concept faded away in the 1990s, leaving a mixed T1/1A fleet as its legacy.

The Hawk had delivered excellent training for Phantom, Harrier, Jaguar and Tornado pilots, but graduates moving on to Typhoon lacked glass cockpit experience. The twin-engined fighter is considerably more expensive to fly than a Hawk, but students were consuming hours simply learning how to work in a modern cockpit. There were clearly advantages to be had by

fielding a new trainer, with a glass cockpit and advanced avionics that could download training from the OCU.

Hawker Siddeley had been absorbed into British Aerospace in 1977, the latter beginning work on the advanced Hawk 100 long before it became part of BAE Systems in 1999. With its more powerful engine, new wing and dramatically revised airframe, the Hawk 100 was an obvious basis for a next-generation RAF Hawk and in 2004 the MoD contracted for 24 examples of the RAF-specific Hawk Mk 128, known in service as the Hawk T.Mk 2.

The aircraft became operational as part of a comprehensive, world-class fast jet training system under the auspices of the new Advanced Fast Jet Training (AFJT) programme, a pioneering component of the wider UK Military Flying Training System that is now reaching fruition. The type served in 19(R) Sqn markings from 2009, changing to IV(R) Sqn colours when the unit renumbered in 2011. Since then, the T2 and wider training system at RAF Valley have proven exceptional, the jet delivering all the capability asked of it and enabling even more capacity to be downloaded from 29(R) Sqn's Typhoons than had been expected. ⊙

Service Variants

Designation	First Delivery	Status
Hawk T.Mk 1	November 4, 1976	Operational
Hawk T.Mk 1A	1983	Operational
Hawk T.Mk 2	2009	Operational

Two Hawk T2s were specially marked for IV(R) Sqn's centenary in 2012. Cpl Peter Devine/© UK MoD Crown Copyright 2017

Airbus Helicopters
H135 Juno

TYPE HISTORY: In 1988, MBB flew the BO108 technology demonstrator with the ultimate aim of replacing the highly successful BO105 in its helicopter line-up. DASA bought MBB the following year, flying a further prototype in 1991, although the design was subsequently altered quite dramatically, including provision of a fenestron in place of the conventional tail rotor.

Now under Eurocopter control after Aerospatiale and DASA merged their helicopter divisions, prototypes of what had become the EC135 flew for the first time on February 15 and April 16, 1994. First customer deliveries followed in July 1996, since when the type has undergone considerable evolution and found favour with a host of civilian, military and para-military customers. After consolidation within the EADS and Airbus groups, Eurocopter became Airbus Helicopters on January 17, 2014.

Among its most successful products, the latest H135 standard offers exceptional performance yet remains the quietest helicopter in its class. The type was included alongside the larger H145 in the UK MFTS rotary wing training package offered by Ascent as the current DHFS provision neared contract end. With Ascent chosen for UK MFTS helicopter training early in 2016, some 29 H135s and three H145s were contracted from Airbus Helicopters in Germany, for completion and initial instructor training in the UK.

The first helicopter had reached the UK before year-end and a pair of H135s and an H145 arrived at RAF Shawbury on April 3, 2017. Release to service was issued on May 12 and the first H135 course is likely to begin in spring 2018. The aircraft has been named Juno. ⊙

ROLE: The Airbus Helicopters H135 Juno has been procured to replace the Squirrel HT1 in the basic rotary wing training role with the Defence Helicopter Flying School at RAF Shawbury. It is expected to begin student courses in 2018.

CAPABILITY: With all but a handful of the UK's frontline military helicopters

The first Juno initially wore German test registration D-HECV, before becoming G-CJIW on the UK civil register. It is serialled ZM504 in service. Steve Hampson

equipped with glass cockpits, the H135 will bring helicopter training into the modern era. It will also ensure continuity and a logical progression for students through the UK Military Flying Training System.

Specification

Airbus Helicopters H135 Juno	
Powerplant	two Safran Helicopter Engines Arrius 2B2^{plus} turboshafts
Length overall	39ft 8½in (12.10m)
Height	12ft 3½in (3.75m)
Maximum take-off weight	6,570lb (2,980kg)
Maximum speed	140kt (278km/h)
Maximum range	329nm (609km)
Hovering ceiling in ground effect	12,700ft

Service Operators

Unit	Type	First Delivery
DHFS	H135 Juno	April 3, 2017

Service Variants

Designation	First Delivery	Status
H135 Juno	April 3, 2017	Due to begin student courses in 2018

A Juno on the ramp at RAF Shawbury marks the beginning of the future of UK military helicopter flying training. WO Charles Williams/© UK MoD Crown Copyright 2017

A Jupiter leads a Juno in to land at RAF Shawbury as the types arrive at their new base for the first time on April 3. The aircraft are superficially similar, thanks to their common forward fuselage architecture, but the Jupiter is somewhat larger and features a prominent fin beneath its fenestron. Ian Forshaw/© UK MoD Crown Copyright 2017

Service Operators

Unit	Type	First Delivery
DHFS/60(R) Sqn	H145 Jupiter	April 3, 2017
DHFS/202(R) Sqn	H145 Jupiter	

Airbus Helicopters
H145 Jupiter

Specification

Airbus Helicopters H145 Jupiter	
Powerplant	two Safran Helicopter Engines Arriel 2E turboshafts rated at 771shp continuous power
Length overall	44ft 9in (13.64m)
Height	13ft 1½in (4m)
Maximum take-off weight	8,157lb (3,700kg)
Never exceed speed	143kt (265km/h)
Maximum range	352nm (651km)
Hovering ceiling in ground effect	12,550ft

ROLE: The Airbus Helicopters H145 Jupiter will replace the Bell Griffin HT.Mk 1 in the advanced rotary wing flying training role from spring 2018.

CAPABILITY: Like the H135, the H145 will introduce digital technology to the helicopter training programme. The Juno and Jupiter cockpits include the very latest in Airbus Helicopters avionics, debuting the manufacturer's new Helionix suite, which delivers enhanced safety and improved situational awareness.

TYPE HISTORY: Germany's MBB and Japan's Kawasaki joined forces in 1977 to design and build the BK117, a twin-engined multi-role helicopter notably equipped with twin clamshell loading doors in its aft fuselage. The first prototype completed its maiden flight on June 13, 1979 and deliveries began in 1983.

DASA and subsequently Eurocopter continued the co-operation with Kawasaki, producing a range of improved variants before embarking upon design of a new helicopter in 1997. This combined the BK117's rear section and cabin with the cockpit and forward section of the EC135, creating a new-generation BK117 equivalent that was designated EC145 from 1999.

Further variants followed, including the dramatically redesigned EC145T2, which emerged in 2011 equipped with Arriel 2E turboshafts and a fenestron. This aircraft forms the basis of the current production H145, which in its latest version includes Helionix avionics, for which Ascent is the first customer. All three H145 Jupiter helicopters ordered against the UK MFTS requirement had been delivered by May 2017. ⊙

Service Variants

Designation	First Delivery	Status
H145 Jupiter	April 3, 2017	Due to begin student courses in 2018

Airbus Helicopters prepared the UK MFTS helicopters at its Oxford Airport base after their delivery form Germany. Jupiter equipment includes a winch. Steve Hampson/ Airbus Helicopters

Beechcraft King Air B200

TYPE: The Beechcraft King Air B200 provides multi-engine pilot training, as well as familiarisation and air experience for trainee rear crew, or Weapon Systems Operators (WSOps). Pilot graduates go on to the RAF transport and tanker fleets, as well as the ISTAR community.

CAPABILITY: Two King Air B200 variants are in service, the basic B200, known as the 'Classic' and B200GT – the 'GT'. The Classics have traditional 'steam gauge', or analogue cockpits featuring the dials and switches of an earlier era. As such, they help ease students into the far more complex King Air from the Tutor, which also has an analogue cockpit.

The GT has a glass cockpit and though a few students make the leap directly from Tutor to GT, most experience the GT in the advanced stage of their course. Thanks to its digital cockpit, the GT is more relevant to the Atlas, C-17, Hercules, Sentinel or Voyager that students are most likely to move on to, but the King Air's nominated replacement, the Embraer Phenom, closes the gap between training and frontline even further.

TYPE HISTORY: Beechcraft produced the first King Air prototype by modifying a piston-engined Queen Air with PT6A turboprops and flying it as the King Air 90 on November 21, 1963. The aircraft spawned a number of variants and many examples entered military service – the model remains in production as the C90GTx.

The stretched Model 100 derivative first flew on March 17, 1969, followed by the Model 200 prototype on October 27, 1972. The latter introduced a 'T'-tail configuration, longer wings, increased fuel capacity and other changes. It found widespread favour with military operators, especially the US services, but eventually appeared in service on a global scale. Like the Model 90 and 100 before it, the Model 200, or B200, evolved into a number of variants. With higher weights, more power and a revised airframe, the Model 300 flew for the first time on October 6, 1981 and although it and the subsequent Model 350 might be considered B200 replacements, the King Air

250 remains in production alongside the King Air 350i and 350ER.

In 2003, Serco was awarded a private finance initiative contract to supply and support seven B200s and provide other facilities to replace 45(R) Sqn's veteran Handley Page Jetstreams in the multi-engine aircrew training role at RAF Cranwell. The initial five-year contract was extended so that Serco continues to supply and maintain the fleet and will do so until the Affinity-supplied Phenom 100 assumes the role around mid-2018. ⊙

Specification

Beechcraft King Air B200GT	
Powerplant	two 850shp Pratt & Whitney Canada PT6A-52 turboprops
Length	43ft 9½in (13.36m)
Height	14ft 9½in (4.51m)
Wingspan	54ft 6in (16.61m)
Wing area	303sqft (28.15m²)
Maximum take-off weight	around 12,500lb (5,670kg)
Service ceiling	35,000ft

Number 45(R) Sqn marked two King Airs in this special scheme to commemorate its centenary in 2016. This aircraft is a B200GT. © Paul Heasman

Service Operators

Unit	Type	First Delivery
45(R) Sqn	King Air B200	2003
45(R) Sqn	King Air B200GT	2003

Service Variants

Designation	First Delivery	Status
King Air B200	2003	Operational
King Air B200GT	2003	Operational

The King Air works well as a trainer, providing a challenging learning environment and good performance, allied with well understood flying qualities. © Paul Heasman

Embraer
Phenom 100

Service Operators

Unit	Type	First Delivery
45(R) Sqn	Phenom 100	

ROLE: The Embraer Phenom 100 is taking over the multi-engine aircrew training duties of the King Air B200 and B200GT. It is expected to begin delivering training in 2018.

CAPABILITY: With its touchscreen cockpit and comprehensive navigation, communications and flight safety suite, the Phenom 100 will deliver a quantum leap in multi-engine flying training. In capability as well as cockpit layout it will be far closer to the frontline types – including Atlas – onto which its students will progress.

TYPE HISTORY: Embraer announced its intention to develop an entry-level business jet in May 2005, beginning the flight test campaign of the unusual Phenom 100 with the prototype's first flight on July 26, 2007. Initially classified as a Very Light Jet, the Phenom was intended for owner-pilot operation, by a single pilot, and therefore featured an extremely comprehensive avionics fit. The cockpit has two seats nonetheless, and the aircraft is

The Phenom 100 combines a distinctive straight wing with a swept 'T'-tail. Combined with state-of-the-art simulation systems, it will revolutionise 45(R) Sqn's training output.
© UK MoD Crown Copyright 2016

capable of taking as many as seven passengers, with cabin access via an airstair door enabling a degree of independence from ground support equipment.

First delivery came in December 2008 and in 2011, Embraer opened a second Phenom production line at Melbourne, Florida. In 2016 this facility became the sole source of Phenom 100 and Phenom 300 aircraft. The latter is a

Service Variants

Designation	First Delivery	Status
Phenom 100	2017	Due to begin student courses in 2018

larger, quite different aircraft related to the Phenom 100 in little but name.

The Phenom 100 quickly found a market beyond that of owner operators and has been accepted as the classic entry-level jet. It has also found favour with airline training departments, particularly those of Emirates and Etihad, setting a precedent that Affinity followed when it sourced five Phenom 100s to satisfy the future multi-engine training requirements laid down under UK MFTS.

Built in Melbourne, but delivered through Embraer's military facility in Brazil, the first RAF Phenom 100 arrived at Cranwell in July, with the second arriving on August 15. Student training is expected to begin in 2018. ◉

Specification

Embraer Phenom 100	
Powerplant	two 1,695lb st (7.54kN) Pratt & Whitney Canada PW617F turbofan engines
Length	42ft 1in (12.82m)
Height	14ft 3in (4.35m)
Wingspan	40ft 4in (12.30m)
High speed cruise	405kt (750km/h)
Range with four occupants and reserves	1,178nm (2,182km)
Maximum operating altitude	41,000ft

This image and above: **All Phenoms are built in Florida, where this RAF example had been rolled out early in 2017. The Service has flown the Shorts Tucano, a licence-built Embraer design, for many years.** © UK MoD Crown Copyright 2016

Boeing
P-8A Poseidon

ROLE: Boeing's P-8A Poseidon is a multi-role maritime patrol aircraft, equipped with sensors and weapons systems for anti-submarine warfare, as well as surveillance and search and rescue missions.

CAPABILITY: The P-8A's comprehensive mission system features an APY-10 radar with modes for high-resolution mapping, an acoustic sensor system, including passive and multi-static sonobuoys, electro-optical/IR turret and electronic support measures (ESM). This equipment delivers comprehensive search and tracking capability, while the aircraft's weapons system includes torpedoes for engaging sub-surface targets.

TYPE HISTORY: Boeing announced the availability of its new Model 737 short/medium-range airliner in 1964. The aircraft struggled to gain orders and Boeing launched into its development programme on little more than hope. The first 737-100 prototype completed its maiden flight on April 9, 1967 and having solved a series of problems, Boeing managed to sell only 30 – the airlines wanted greater capacity. The stretched 737-200 was the aircraft they needed and the 737's success since has been astronomic.

This US Navy Poseidon was at RAF Lossiemouth on July 13, when the RAF ISTAR Force Commander announced the numbers allocated to the two future P-8 squadrons. SAC Charlotte Hopkins/© UK MoD Crown Copyright 2017

The first major change in the line came with the CFM56 turbofan, which replaced the original Pratt & Whitney JT8D from 1984. In response to continuous improvements in the Airbus A320, Boeing reworked the 737 again, as the 737 Next Generation (NG), with a new wing, full-authority digital engine control (FADEC) and other improvements. Among the NG variants, Boeing selected the 737-800 as the basis of its P-8A Poseidon submission to replace the veteran Lockheed P-3 Orion in US Navy service.

A contract for P-8 development was granted in June 2004 and first flight followed on April 25, 2009. The US Navy announced initial operating capability on November 29, 2013 and the P-8 is now been widely delivered not only to US units, but also to the Indian Navy and Royal Australian Air Force.

The BAE Systems Nimrod MRA.Mk 4 upgrade of existing Nimrod MR.Mk 2

Service Operators

Unit	Type	First Delivery
120 Sqn	P-8A Poseidon	April 2018
201 Sqn	P-8A Poseidon	2021

Service Variants

Designation	First Delivery	Status
P-8A Poseidon	2020	

airframes had been underway for some years when it was axed under the 2010 Strategic Defence and Security Review. The MR.Mk 2 was also withdrawn, leaving the UK without effective long-range, fixed-wing maritime cover. Project Seedcorn saw personnel posted into maritime patrol units with allied air arms, maintaining vital skills until the 2015 Strategic Defence and Security Review confirmed the intended purchase of nine Poseidons for the RAF.

With the P-8 squadron numbers chosen, the type will operate from RAF Lossiemouth, where infrastructure is being prepared for its arrival around 2020. The aircraft will be equipped with US weapons, although British weapons may be integrated in future. ◉

Specification

Boeing P-8A Poseidon	
Powerplant	two 27,000lb st (120kN) CFM International CFM56-7 turbofan engines
Length	129ft 6in (39.47m)
Height	42ft 1¼in (12.83m)
Wingspan	123ft 7¼in (37.64m)
Maximum take-off weight	189,200lb (85,820kg)
Maximum speed	490kt (907km/h)
Ferry range	4,500 miles (7,242km)
Service ceiling	41,000ft

As this VP-45, US Navy crew demonstrates, the P-8 features a modern glass cockpit. Lt jg Keith Estes/US Navy

Airbus Helicopters
Puma HC

C.Mk 2

ROLE: The Puma HC.Mk 2 medium support helicopter operates under Joint Helicopter Command (JHC) control. The aircraft is used in a variety of combat roles, including the tactical movement of troops, weapons, ammunition and stores on the battlefield, as well as the extraction of casualties and in response to medical emergencies on the frontline. It is also employed during non-combatant evacuations, and humanitarian and disaster relief operations.

Exercise Jebel Sahara in 2015 provided an opportunity for Puma Force to prove the hot-and-high capability of the new Mk 2 helicopter. Cpl Connor Payne/© UK MoD Crown Copyright 2017

No further evidence of the transformation in Puma performance is required than its success on Operation Toral, supporting the continued Coalition presence in Afghanistan, where this 33 Sqn aircraft was demonstrating its ability to launch flares to decoy infrared-homing missiles. Cpl Alex Scott/© UK MoD Crown Copyright 2017

Below right: **Regular exercises keep the Puma squadrons sharp and ready to deploy. Like Chinook Force, the Pumas work closely with the British Army, and these Puma HC2s were on exercise with Army units on Salisbury Plain.** Sgt Mitch Moore/© UK MoD Crown Copyright 2017

CAPABILITY:

The aircraft is capable of carrying 16 passengers, 12 fully equipped troops or up to 2 tonnes of freight, the latter moved as internal cargo or underslung, or a mix of the two. It can also be fitted with up to six stretchers for operations in the casualty evacuation or medical emergency response team role.

With more powerful engines, greater range than the Puma HC.Mk 1 and a modern digital cockpit, the Puma HC.Mk 2 is capable of operating in harsh environments, lifting troops, supplies and humanitarian aid wherever needed, especially under hot-and-high conditions. The aircraft can be prepared for transport by C-17 in just four hours, flown across the globe, and be rebuilt and returned to flying just as quickly at the destination, making it a highly mobile, deployable battlefield support helicopter.

TYPE HISTORY:

In 1967, France and the UK reached agreement over a joint helicopter development programme in which their two industries would create three rotary types. Sud-Aviation in France had developed its SA300 design as a medium transport helicopter in 1965 and this formed the basis of the SA330 Puma, to be built on production lines in France (by Sud-Aviation, and Aerospatiale from 1970) and the UK (by Westland). The other types involved were the Aerospatiale Gazelle and Westland Lynx.

An SA330 was delivered to the UK in 1968 and Westland subsequently built 48 to Puma HC.Mk 1 standard, flying its initial example for the first time on November 25, 1970. The type entered service with 33 Sqn in June the following year and with 230 Sqn in January 1972. Replacing the Westland Whirlwind HC.Mk 10 in what was then the army support role and is

now regarded as the support helicopter task, the Puma saw its first major operational service monitoring ceasefire arrangements in Rhodesia during 1980.

It also served extensively in Northern Ireland, and in Belize during tensions with neighbouring Guatemala, where it provided mobility for the British Army and support for RAF Harriers. The Puma also provided essential lift during Operation Granby, the British contribution to Operations Desert Shield and Desert Storm, which successfully liberated Kuwait from Iraqi occupation in 1991.

Later action saw the Puma working over the former Yugoslavia and engaged in humanitarian efforts around the world. In three decades of

Service Variants

Designation	First Delivery	Status
Puma HC.Mk 1	June 1971	24 aircraft upgraded to HC.Mk 2 standard
Puma HC.Mk 2	2013	Operational

service, the aircraft had changed remarkably little, save for the addition of specific role equipment and simple self protection systems, but when the UK committed forces to Operation Herrick in Afghanistan, its limitations at last became apparent.

Most importantly, the helicopter lacked power in the hot-and-high conditions typical of the Afghan summer, and in its mountains, leaving it short of lift and largely unsuitable for sustained deployment. Instead the Puma gave sterling service working with troops preparing to deploy on the various Herrick rotations, providing them with experience of helicopter operations in the relatively benign conditions of a training exercise.

But the Puma's continued utility was potentially great, particularly its ability to provide considerable capability with minimal footprint, which makes it ideal for operations in urban areas. It was therefore decided that a dramatic upgrade should be applied to 24 airframes, providing them with the Makila 1A1 turboshaft of the Super Puma, advanced digital avionics and more fuel capacity, among other significant changes.

Eurocopter undertook the work, having taken design responsibility from Aerospatiale, delivering the first Puma HC.Mk 2 back to RAF Benson for operational trials in 2013; the type is now the responsibility of Airbus Helicopters. Crews immediately appreciated its radically improved performance and the broad situational awareness provided by its avionics, especially when the Puma returned to full operational service in 2015. It remains a key support helicopter asset with 33 and 230 Sqns, both of them long-term Puma operators, and the unusual 28 Sqn, which flies the Puma and Chinook as the support helicopter OCU.

Thanks in part to its compact dimensions, the Puma is rapidly and easily air transportable, making it an ideal choice for early deployment into disaster or combat zones. Cpl Connor Payne/© UK MoD Crown Copyright 2017

Service Operators

Unit	Type	Operational Capability with Mk 2
28 Sqn	Puma HC.Mk 2	2015
33 Sqn	Puma HC.Mk 2	June 2015
230 Sqn	Puma HC.Mk 2	June 2015

Externally the HC2 is virtually identical to the Puma Mk 1, but the change in the cockpit is profound, from 1960s-vintage dials and switches to multi-function displays. Sgt Mitch Moore/© UK MoD Crown Copyright 2017

Specification

Airbus Helicopters Puma HC.Mk 2	
Powerplant	two 1,800shp Turbomeca Makila 1A1 turboshaft engines
Length overall	59ft 8½in (18.20m)
Height	16ft 10½in (5.14m)
Main rotor diameter	49ft 6in (15.09m)
Maximum speed	167kt (309km/h)
Payload	up to 16 passengers, 12 fully equipped troops or 4,400lb (2,000kg) of freight
Armament	two 7.62mm GPMGs

Grob 120TP
Prefect

ROLE: Under the new UK MFTS construct, the Grob 120TP Prefect is replacing the Tutor T1 in the elementary flying training Role with 57(R) Sqn at RAF College Cranwell.

CAPABILITY: Nominally based at Cranwell but operating out of nearby RAF Barkston Heath, the Prefect brings turboprop power, digital avionics and retractable undercarriage to elementary flying training. These features make it entirely relevant to the next stage in UK MFTS, whether students progress to the Juno helicopter, Texan II basic trainer or Phenom multi-engine platform. It will eliminate the need for students to learn glass cockpit flying later in their training and establish a digital precedent all the way to the frontline.

TYPE HISTORY: Grob's 120TP is an extreme evolution of a line of two-seat sporting and aerobatic aircraft that began with the Grob G 115, first flown in 1985 and including the G 115E, ordered in quantity for UK service as the Tutor. First flown in 2010, the 120TP employs a composite airframe and turboprop power, plus digital avionics and a glass cockpit.

Affinity is supplying 23 Prefects under UK MFTS and having been contracted on February 2, 2016, received its first pair of aircraft on November 16. The fleet built rapidly and the type was ready to begin operations on August 1, 2017. With five machines on the ramp at Barkston Heath, Sqn Ldr Balshaw, from the RAF Central Flying School, and Ascent Chief Pilot Nigel Scopes took off from Barkston Heath for the first training flight of a new UKMFTS machine since the Hawk T2 entered service in 2009. ☉

Service Operators

Unit	Type	First UK MFTS Sortie
57(R) Sqn	Prefect	August 1, 2017

Service Variants

Designation	First Delivery	Status
Prefect	November 16, 2016	Operational

Specification

Grob 120TP Prefect	
Powerplant	one Rolls-Royce M250-B17F turboprop engine rated at 380shp maximum continuous power
Length	27ft 7in (8.40m)
Height	8ft 10in (2.70m)
Wingspan	33ft 10in (10.30m)
Wing area	145sqft (13.50m²)
Empty weight	2,414lb (1,095kg)
Maximum take-off weight for aerobatics	3,175lb (1,440kg)
Maximum speed	245kt (454km/h)
Rate of climb	2,855ft/min (870m/min)
Range at 5,000ft and long-range cruising speed	640nm (1,185km)
Maximum operating altitude	25,000ft

For UK MFTS service, the 120TP has been named Prefect after the Avro Prefect, a navigation trainer that flew alongside the Avro Tutor elementary trainer during the 1930s. Jamie Hunter/Aviacom

The large turret under Reaper's forward fuselage contains electro-optical sensors and a laser designator. The bulbous fairing above covers the main satellite communications antenna, linking the aircraft back to its GCS. Sgt Ross Tilly/© UK MoD Crown Copyright 2017

General Atomics
MQ-9A Reaper

ROLE: The MQ-9 Reaper is a remotely piloted medium-altitude, long endurance (MALE) aircraft designed for Intelligence, Surveillance, Target Acquisition and Reconnaissance (ISTAR), and attack missions. The aircraft's persistence and array of surveillance sensors are an essential complement to the RAF's crewed platforms.

CAPABILITY: A crew comprising a pilot, sensor operator and mission intelligence co-ordinator flies Reaper from a remote ground control station (GCS). An in-theatre launch and recovery team is responsible for its ground operations. The operational crew controls the aircraft, its sensors and weapons system via an advanced, secure satellite communication system, providing over-the-horizon data link capability from bases in the UK and US.

Two cameras in the aircraft's forward fuselage provide a forward view for the crew on landing and take-off, while a full sensor suite, with targeting, daylight TV and infrared capabilities

is turret mounted beneath Reaper's forward fuselage. An internal synthetic aperture radar completes the MQ-9's sensor suite.

TYPE HISTORY: The US military has been using unmanned air vehicles (UAVs), also known as remotely piloted air systems (RPAS) or, popularly, drones, for intelligence gathering since the 1960s. In December 1984, a new avenue of development began when the Defense Advanced Research Projects Agency began a programme to develop a series of small, multi-role UAVs. The programme was known as Amber and Leading Systems Inc (LSI) created several Amber prototypes under its direction, flying the first in 1986.

Initially powered by engines of just 65hp, the Amber prototypes paved the way for LSI to begin development of the Gnat 750, suitable for sale on the export market. Still limited by the 65hp of its Rotax piston engine, the Gnat 750 looked remarkably like a half-scale Reaper.

General Atomics purchased LSI before the Gnat entered production, completing the type's first flight in 1989. The Gnat 750, and related I-Gnat and Gnat XP, saw limited service with US agencies until at least well into the 1990s.

By then, General Atomics had advanced with the design of the more powerful, more capable MQ-1 Predator, which it rolled out in August 1994, against a contract awarded only on January 7. Production of a 100hp version for the USAF and US Navy was ordered in August 1997, after a handful of pre-production aircraft had been deployed for service over Bosnia in 1996. The Predator's exceptional surveillance capabilities were immediately evident, but no real effort to equip it with targeting systems or weapons occurred until 2000.

By summer 2001, successful trials with the AGM-114 Hellfire and an onboard targeting system were complete and the Predator had fired missiles in anger against targets in Afghanistan before year-end. While the MQ-1

Above: **This Reaper was approaching to land at Kandahar, Afghanistan, under the control of 39 Sqn at Creech, in November 2010.** Sgt Corinne Buxton/© UK MoD Crown Copyright 2017

was being weaponised, General Atomics was working on a new UAV designated Predator B. The title was, in fact, a misnomer, since the aircraft bore little in common with the MQ-1, apart from its general configuration.

Predator B featured a 900shp TPE331 turboprop and was designed for a heavy payload of sensors and weapons. The USAF committed to the Predator B programme under the designation MQ-9A Reaper. Work on the prototypes was well under way during 2001 and the type became available for operations in 2007.

The RAF's association with Reaper has its origins in 1115 Flight, formed under the Combined Joint Predator Task Force in January 2004. This embedded UK personnel in US Predator operations, providing a core of expertise when Reaper training began in December 2006. Operations in Afghanistan began in 2007, 39 Sqn working out of Creech Air Force Base, Nevada with an initial six aircraft, although one of these was subsequently lost.

Five additional aircraft were contracted in 2012 and on October 26, XIII Sqn re-formed in preparation for operations from RAF Waddington. Reaper had been scheduled to go out of service in 2015, but has since been heavily committed to Operation Shader. The 2015 Strategic Defence and Security Review confirmed that a replacement RPAS would be sort to include more than 20 aircraft for delivery from 2018.

In April 2016 the MoD announced selection of Protector, based on the Certifiable Predator B, to replace Reaper, while US State Department approval provides for as many as 26 airframes, as 16 confirmed and ten options. New GCS will also be acquired and UK weapons could be integrated. ⊙

Right: **Taxiing out for a mission from Kandahar, this Reaper is armed with four Hellfires.** Sgt Ross Tilly/© UK MoD Crown Copyright 2017

A three-person crew operates Reaper, working from a remote GCS. Sgt Andrew Morris/© UK MoD Crown Copyright 2017

Specification

General Atomics MQ-9A Reaper	
Powerplant	one 900shp Honeywell TPE331-10 turboprop
Length	36ft (10.97m)
Height	12ft (3.66m)
Wingspan	69ft 3½in (21.12m)
Maximum take-off weight	10,500lb (4,760kg)
Maximum speed	250kt (463km/h)
Endurance (clean)	20 hours
Endurance (with weapons)	more than 12 hours
Service ceiling (clean)	more than 50,000ft
Service ceiling (with weapons)	more than 30,000ft
Armament	two 500lb GBU-12 laser-guided bombs and four AGM-114 Hellfire missiles

Service Variants

Designation	First Delivery	Status
RQ-9A Reaper	2007	Operational

Service Operators

Unit	Type	First Delivery
XIII Sqn	RQ-9A Reaper	April 24, 2013
39 Sqn	RQ-9A Reaper	July 2007

Raytheon
Sentinel R.Mk 1

ROLE: The Sentinel R.Mk 1 provides long-range, wide-area battlefield surveillance, delivering critical intelligence and target tracking information to British and coalition forces. The aircraft has been operationally deployed in support of operations in Afghanistan, Libya and Mali, and is currently deployed in support of British and Coalition operations in Iraq and Syria.

CAPABILITY: Using Its powerful multi-mode radar, the Sentinel's mission crew identifies, tracks and images numerous targets over great ranges, passing the information in near real time to friendly forces. A team of intelligence imagery analysts from 1 Intelligence, Surveillance, Reconnaissance (ISR) Wing backs up the Sentinel crews, conducting in-depth forensic analysis of collected data, and using it to generate intelligence products for time-critical dissemination to commanders and decision makers, enabling them to execute current operations and plan future strategies.

Right: **Engine start for a Sentinel temporarily based at RAF Akrotiri. The aircraft was preparing for an Operation Shader mission on July 31.** Cpl Graham Taylor/© UK MoD Crown Copyright 2017

Below: **Externally, the Sentinel's major identifiers are the massive 'canoe' radome covering the radar antenna under its forward fuselage and the large fairing above.** Sgt Laura Bibby/© UK MoD Crown Copyright 2017

Service Variants

Designation	First Delivery	Status
Sentinel R.Mk 1	2007	Operational

Service Operators

Unit	Type	First Delivery
V(AC) Sqn	Sentinel R.Mk 1	2008

Above: **Although home based at RAF Waddington, the Sentinel is frequently deployed overseas. The type flew 14,000 hours on Operation Herrick between November 2008 and November 2014.** © UK MoD Crown Copyright 2017

Above: **The Sentinel's business jet origins ensure excellent range and altitude performance. Inside, however, the aircraft is packed with operator stations and mission systems, with none of the comfort expected from a private jet.** © UK MoD Crown Copyright 2017

Below: **As well as its essential work overseas, V(AC) Sqn has used the Sentinel's unique sensor capability at home. Its radar was put to good use generating images showing the extent of flooding in the Thames Valley during January 2014.** © UK MoD Crown Copyright 2017

TYPE HISTORY: During the early 1980s, the UK government identified a need for a battlefield reconnaissance system to provide awareness over a broad area. Expressed in the Corps Airborne Stand-Off Radar (CASTOR) requirement, the programme elicited responses from Thorn-EMI and Ferranti. The former's radar was tested in an English Electric Canberra from 1982, while a Britten-Norman Islander modified to take the latter, first flew in 1984.

By 1988 the programme had become ASTOR and, with a Thorn-EMI radar installed, the Islander flew low-altitude trials examining its compatibility with the USAF's prototype E-8 J-STARS (Joint-Surveillance Target Acquisition Radar System). This work was part of a definition phase which, it was hoped, would enable a contract award in 1994.

Finally, in 1999, Raytheon was contracted to develop a five-aircraft ASTOR system, using Bombardier's Global Express business jet as the airborne platform and basing the mission system on its ASARS-2 radar, developed for the USAF's U-2. Raytheon took a first Global

Specification

Raytheon Sentinel R.Mk 1	
Powerplant	two 14,750lb st (65.60kN) Rolls-Royce Deutschland BR710 turbofan engines
Length	99ft 5in (30.30m)
Height	27ft (8.23m)
Wingspan	93ft 5½in (28.49m)
Wing area	1,022sqft (94.95m²)
Maximum speed	530kt (982km/h)
Range	more than 5,000nm (9,260km)
Maximum altitude	more than 40,000ft

Express for modification in 2002 and re-flew it with the ASTOR system installed in May 2004. Service trials began in 2007 and V(AC) Sqn flew the first operational Sentinel R.Mk 1 mission in November 2008.

The aircraft immediately proved its worth over Afghanistan and again during Operation Ellamy in 2011, becoming a vital link in the chain of target identification and prosecution, especially where fleeting or 'pop-up' targets were concerned. The 2010 Strategic Defence and Security Review nominated Sentinel for withdrawal as soon as the Operation Herrick commitment ended, but such was the system's value to British and allied commanders that it was given a reprieve. Since then it continues to prove its worth in Operation Shader and as a result of the 2015 Strategic Defence and Security Review, its out of service date has been moved back to 2021. ◉

Beechcraft
Shadow R.Mk 1

Right: **A comprehensive antenna farm on the upper fuselage serves the Shadow's communications suite, with sensors mounted on the fuselage underside.** © UK MoD Crown Copyright 2017

Main Image: **Shadow incorporates a comprehensive mission suite into a King Air 350 airframe.** Cpl Steve Buckley/ © UK MoD Crown Copyright 2017

Specification

Beechcraft Shadow R.Mk 1	
Powerplant	two 850shp Pratt & Whitney Canada PT6A-47A turboprop engines
Length	43ft 9¼in (13.34m)
Height	15ft (4.57m)
Wingspan	54ft 6in (16.61m)
Wing area	310sqft (28.80m²)
Maximum cruising speed	294kt (544km/h)
Maximum altitude	35,000ft

Service Operators

Unit	Type	First Delivery
14 Sqn	Shadow R.Mk 1	2011

Service Variants

Designation	First Delivery	Status
Shadow R.Mk 1	2009	Operational

ROLE: Through a combination of sensors, Shadow adds a comprehensive intelligence gathering capability to ISTAR Force. Its output is particularly valuable to ground commanders.

CAPABILITY: The Shadow's electro-optical and electronic capabilities complement those of the Sentinel R.Mk 1, its data combining with that gathered by Sentinel and other platforms to help analysts prepare comprehensive intelligence product. Satellite communications links enable information download during a mission and the aircraft is also fitted with a comprehensive defensive aids suite.

TYPE HISTORY: The US has been using variants of the ubiquitous King Air twin-turboprop business aircraft in military roles since the early 1960s, subsequently creating and fielding a family of Guardrail reconnaissance machines based on the King Air 200.

Originally a Beechcraft product, subsequently marketed as Beech and then Hawker Beechcraft under Raytheon ownership, and now regarded as a Beechcraft product under Textron Aviation, the King Air has most recently been developed into the King Air 350. More capable than earlier versions, the King Air 350 was offered as a special missions platform from the outset and spawned the new generation MC-12 ISR platform ordered for the US Air Force in July 2008 against an urgent need to improve intelligence gathering in Afghanistan.

A similar requirement led the RAF to commission an initial four Shadow R.Mk 1 aircraft, based on the King Air 350CER, under an urgent operational requirement. Delivered to V(AC) Sqn in 2009, the Shadow features an underfuselage electro-optical sensor turret, a variety of integrated sensors and extensive communications capability, managed from operator consoles in the cabin.

Number V(AC) Sqn's Shadow flight became 14 Sqn in 2011, after the former Tornado unit disbanded at RAF Lossiemouth under the 2010 Strategic Defence and Security Review. A fifth aircraft, plus a dedicated trainer were added to the fleet and the aircraft's exceptional performance has seen it identified as a key asset for the future.

The 2015 Strategic Defence and Security Review called for the trainer to receive a roll-on/roll-off mission suite that might enable its use in operational and training roles, plus the addition of two new airframes. The first of these three is likely to be in service from 2019 and the expanded fleet should remain operational until at last 2030. ●

The Squirrel has provided excellent service, but is being replaced by the thoroughly modern Juno. Airbus Helicopters now has design authority for the AS350, which is no longer in production. Ian Forshaw/© UK MoD Crown Copyright 2017

Airbus Helicopters
Squirrel HT.Mk 1

ROLE: The Defence Helicopter Flying School (DHFS) at RAF Shawbury uses the Squirrel HT.Mk 1 to deliver elementary rotary-wing flying training. The aircraft has a secondary liaison/light transport role.

CAPABILITY: The Squirrel HT.Mk 1 (and HT.Mk 2 in Army Air Corps (AAC) service) delivers UK military Single Engine Basic Rotary Wing (SEBRW) training under the auspices of 660 Sqn, AAC and 705 NAS, within the DHFS. The Squirrel has proven an ideal platform to teach the primary skills of rotary wing flying, but its analogue cockpit is no longer representative of the majority of frontline helicopter types onto which graduates will eventually progress.

The basic phase of the SEBRW course teaches general handling, including emergency procedures, while the advanced phase includes instrument flying, medium- and low-level navigation, operating into confined areas, reversionary night flying, formation and mountain flying. The Central Flying School (Helicopter) Squadron at RAF Shawbury uses the Squirrel to train instructors, while 670 Sqn, AAC at Middle Wallop employs it in the operational training phase of Army pilot training.

As well as these core training tasks, Squirrel crews conduct a variety of liaison and communications flying, including transporting senior officers and route reconnaissance for Joint Helicopter Command units. There is also a standing commitment to support the Royal Air Force Aerobatic Team The Red Arrows during the display season, when a Squirrel is used to move Red 10, the team's safety officer and commentator, between show venues.

TYPE HISTORY: Aerospatiale flew the initial AS350 Ecureuil prototype on June 27, 1974 as the first step in bringing a replacement for the Sud-Aviation Alouette III to market. The aircraft was developed along parallel lines, employing either Lycoming or Turbomeca Arriel power, the AS350B featuring the latter engine. The more powerful AS350B2 featured enlarged main rotor blades for increased maximum take-off weight, gaining certification in 1989. A large range of single and twin-engined variants followed.

Service Operators

Unit	Type	Service Entry
DHFS	Squirrel HT.Mk 1	April 1997

Service Variants

Designation	Service Entry	Status
Squirrel HT.Mk 1	April 1997	Operational

Specification

Airbus Helicopters Squirrel HT.Mk 1	
Powerplant	one 625shp Safran Helicopter Engines Arriel 1D1 turboshaft
Length overall, rotors turning	42ft 5½in (12.94m)
Height overall	10ft 3½in (3.14m)
Main rotor diameter	35ft ¾in (10.69m)
Main rotor disc area	966.10sqft (89.75m²)
Maximum take-off weight	4,960lb (2,250kg)
Never exceed speed at sea level	155kt (287km/h)
Maximum rate of climb at sea level	1,752ft/min (534m/min)
Maximum range	362nm (670km)
Hovering ceiling in ground effect	10,500ft

In 1996, FB Heliservices assumed responsibility for supplying aircraft and availability for the Defence Helicopter Flying School at RAF Shawbury, under a private finance initiative. It ordered 38 AS350BB helicopters from what was now Eurocopter, plus nine Bell 412s from the US manufacturer. Based on the AS350B2, the 'BB' was modified specifically for the UK requirement and delivered from November 1996. Twenty-six aircraft were to Squirrel HT.Mk 1 standard, the remainder to Mk 2 specification, with cockpits equipped for NVGs.

FB Heliservices, a Flight Refuelling Aviation (now Cobham) and Bristow joint venture, has continued with the contract, but responsibility for the DHFS fleet will pass to Ascent in 2018, using the Juno and Jupiter helicopters. ○

Beechcraft
T-6C Texan II

ROLE: The Beechcraft T-6C Texan II will take over the basic fast jet training role currently fulfilled by the Tucano T.Mk 1. Students will progress onto the aircraft from the Prefect and move forwards to the Hawk T2.

CAPABILITY: Continuing the precedent set by the Tucano for employing a tandem-seat turboprop basic trainer, the Texan II replaces the analogue cockpit of the earlier machine with a digital glass cockpit featuring modern avionics. The aircraft's mission system is capable of generating simulated air-to-air targets and scoring against the release of simulated air-to-ground ordnance.

TYPE HISTORY: Under Raytheon ownership, Beech developed the T-6A Texan II from the Pilatus PC-9, in response to the long-running US Joint Primary Aircraft Training System (JPATS) requirement to replace the Cessna T-37. After reworking a Pilatus-supplied airframe, Beech flew a production standard Texan II, known then as the Beech Mk II, for the first time in December 1992. On June 22, 1995 Beech was announced winner of the JPATS competition and the Texan II began re-equipping USAF flying training squadrons in May 2000.

The Texan II name recalls the North American T-6 Texan of World War II, a type used extensively by the RAF and Royal Canadian Air Force as the Harvard. When the T-6A-1 was developed as the CT-156 for the NATO Flying Training in Canada programme, it was appropriately named Harvard II. Subsequent variants include the T-6B for the US Navy and T-6C export version.

Chosen to supply a Tucano replacement under UK MFTS, Affinity is sourcing ten T-6C Texan II aircraft from Beechcraft, which is now a Textron company. The first aircraft built against the order completed its maiden flight in May and visited the UK to appear at the Royal International Air Tattoo in July.

The Texan II will initially be stationed at RAF Linton-on-Ouse, which has long since housed the Tucano, but will later be based at RAF Valley alongside the Hawk T2. Training on the new turboprop is expected to begin early in 2019. ⊙

Service Operators

Unit	Type	First Student Course Expected
	T-6C Texan II	2019

Service Variants

Designation	First Flight of a UK Aircraft	Status
T-6C Texan II	May 2017	Due to begin student courses in 2019

Affinity's first T-6C completed its maiden flight, in British markings, during May 2017.
Affinity

Specification

Beechcraft T-6C Texan II	
Powerplant	one 1,100shp Pratt & Whitney Canada PT6A turboprop engine
Length	33ft 4in (10.16m)
Height	10ft 8in (3.25m)
Wingspan	33ft 5in (10.20m)
Wing area:	175.30sqft (16.28m²)
Maximum take-off weight	6,900lb (3,130kg)
Maximum speed	316kt (585km/h)
Ferry range	884nm (1,637km)
Maximum altitude	31,000ft

Panavia
Tornado GR.Mk 4

ROLE: The Panavia Tornado GR.Mk 4 is the UK's primary ground attack platform and also fulfils an important reconnaissance role. The aircraft conducts attack missions against planned targets, armed reconnaissance against targets of opportunity and close air support (CAS) for ground forces, typically under the control of a Joint Terminal Attack Controller (JTAC).

For attacks against pre-planned targets the Tornado GR4 usually employs GPS/laser-guided bombs from the Paveway family, or the Storm Shadow cruise missile, the latter fired from considerable stand-off ranges. In the armed reconnaissance and CAS roles, Tornado normally carries a mix of Paveway IV and Dual-Mode Seeker Brimstone, combined with a Litening III targeting pod, and in addition to the internal 27mm gun. This gives the crew an unparalleled array of options to engage targets with the most appropriate weapon, achieving the desired result with minimum, if any, collateral damage.

CAPABILITY: With its mix of weapons, the Tornado GR4 is capable of engaging all targets on the modern battlefield. Paveway III and Storm Shadow afford the ability to strike bunkers and other hardened facilities, while Brimstone is effective against armoured vehicles, both static and on the move. Dual-Mode Seeker Brimstone enables precision strike against targets with collateral-damage challenges; these can be moving at high speed and still successfully engaged.

Paveway IV offers huge tactical flexibility, with cockpit-programmable impact angle, impact direction and fuse delay offering precisely tailored strike on planned and unplanned targets. The 27mm gun offers the ability to strike targets including light vehicles and personnel; it proved invaluable in Afghanistan for halting insurgent ambushes when crews strafed into tree lines.

During Operation Ellamy in 2011, Tornados flew from the UK to strike targets in Libya using Storm Shadow missiles, a round trip of more than 3,000nm, accomplished with essential support from Vickers VC10 and Lockheed TriStar tankers. Some missions saw the Tornados launch their missiles and then turn for Gioia de Colle, Italy, where they joined other Tornados, and Typhoons, in a sustained campaign against Libyan government forces.

Through its unique weapons effects and the RAF's air-to-air refuelling capability, Tornado provides the UK Government with a rapid and flexible crisis response tool.

TYPE HISTORY: Britain's relationship with variable geometry (VG) wing design dates back to the 1950s when Sir Barnes Wallis, better known for developing the Upkeep 'bouncing bomb' used by 617 Sqn 'The Dambusters' in 1943, worked through several VG concepts. Barnes and others recognised that with a VG aircraft's wings swept forwards, or spread, it could use shorter runways and display greater manoeuvrability, before sweeping them back for maximum high-speed performance. From

RAPTOR is a large store, carried under the Tornado's fuselage. The doors in the pod's side slide open to reveal the 'windows' through which its sensors 'see'. The carrier aircraft in this case has a brown-coloured 'window' on its forward fuselage, carried over from its previous GR.Mk 1A incarnation.
SAC Mitch Poole/© UK MoD Crown Copyright 2017

The ability to penetrate enemy air defences at low-altitude and high speed was written into the Tornado's specification at an early stage. It's a tactic that remains relevant and practised today. SAC Tim Laurence/© UK MoD Crown Copyright 2017

Specification

Panavia Tornado GR.Mk 4	
Powerplant	two Turbo-Union RB.199 Mk 103 turbofans each rated at 16,000lb st (71.50kN) with afterburning
Length	56ft 6¼in (17.23m)
Height	19ft 6¼in (5.95m)
Wingspan, spread	45ft 7½in (13.91m)
Wingspan, swept	28ft 1in (8.56m)
Wing area	286.33sqft (26.60m²)
Maximum take-off weight	around 61,600lb (27,950kg)
Maximum speed	Mach 1.3
Armament	Paveway II, III and IV series GPS/laser-guided bombs, Brimstone air-to-ground missiles, Storm Shadow cruise missiles, ASRAAM for self defence, one internal 27mm Mauser cannon, plus 1,500-litre and/or 2,250-litre drop tanks, Litening III targeting pod, RAPTOR, Sky Shadow and BOZ countermeasures pods, up to a maximum disposable load of around 19,840lb (9,000kg)

the 1940s into the early 1970s, VG wings were an excellent solution to difficult aerodynamic and operational challenges, although at a penalty of additional airframe weight compared to fixed wings. The advent of more advanced aerodynamics, and especially of powerful, lightweight computing systems, enabled designers to extract similar performance without the weight and complications of VG.

Although no aircraft were built as a result of Wallis's work, it inspired the British Aircraft Corporation (BAC) P.45 VG fighter-bomber study and subsequent Anglo-French Variable Geometry (AFVG) attack/interceptor concepts, from which France soon withdrew, but the UK continued as UKVG.

Looking for an industrial partner, BAC approached West Germany's MBB, which was on the verge of termination of the Advanced Vertical Strike (AVS) vertical take-off and landing aircraft on which it had worked with US companies. It was already also contemplating a single-seat, single-engined lightweight fighter-bomber as the Neue Kampffluegzeug (NKF). There was some commonality in intended role between

UKVG and NKF, and the difficult process of international collaboration began.

The Luftwaffe's primary requirement for NKF was to replace its Fiat G.91 and Lockheed F-104 Starfighter fleets and since Belgium, Italy and the Netherlands had similar F-104 issues, they joined with West Germany in January 1968 to propose an NKF-informed Multi-Role Aircraft for 1975 (MRA 75). The UKVG had, meanwhile, been replaced by two concepts, one for a light combat aircraft and the other for a heavier, twin-engined design.

In concept the latter was close to MRA 75 and on July 25, 1968, Belgium, Canada, Italy, the Netherlands, West Germany and the UK launched feasibility studies around the requirement. Belgium and Canada soon fell by the wayside since they were primarily looking for an interceptor, but in December, BAC, Italy's Fiat and MBB formed a joint industrial company to formally develop a new aircraft.

BAC and MBB had quite different VG designs in progress, the former focussing on a twin-engined aircraft powered by two new technology RB.199 turbofans, while the MBB concept relied on a single General Electric TF30 engine. Compromise was eventually agreed and the layout for a new Multi-Role Combat Aircraft (MRCA) described in a March 14, 1969 meeting. The joint industrial company formed the previous December became Panavia on March 26 and BAC, MBB, Fiat and VFV-Fokker in the Netherlands began work.

This Tornado demonstrates a typical GR4 fit, with two Paveway IVs (the blue-painted, inert weapons), a single Brimstone under the aft fuselage and a Litening III pod forward. The slim missile under the port wing, inboard of the drop tank, is ASRAAM. Cpl Mike Jones/© UK MoD Crown Copyright 2017

Service Variants

Designation	First Delivery	Status
Tornado GR.Mk 1	July 1, 1980	Withdrawn, some upgraded to GR.Mk 4
Tornado GR.Mk 1A	December 1986	Withdrawn, some upgraded to GR.Mk 4A
Tornado GR.Mk 1B	1993	26 conversions from GR1, some further upgraded to GR.Mk 4
Tornado F.Mk 2	November 5, 1985	Withdrawn from OCU service in 1988
Tornado F.Mk 3	December 1, 1986	Withdrawn in 2011
Tornado GR.Mk 4	1998	Operational
Tornado GR.Mk 4A	1998	Absorbed into GR4 fleet, operational

This GR4 was launching from Akrotiri in February 2017, toting a pair of Storm Shadows for an Operation Shader mission. Cpl Tony Rogers/© UK MoD Crown Copyright 2017

Although a degree of compromise had been reached, Panavia was established to produce a single-seat Panavia 100, primarily for interception duties, and a two-seat Panavia 200, which satisfied the UK requirement for a long-range attack aircraft. Neither specification really suited the Dutch, who needed a multi-role interceptor/attack aircraft, rather than a pure interceptor or heavy, long-range striker and the Netherlands soon withdrew from the programme. In November 1969, Fiat merged with Aerfer to form Aeritalia and it was therefore this new concern, along with BAC and MBB that continued MRCA development, the single-seat requirement fading away during 1970.

A new company was formed to develop the RB.199 turbofan, Fiat, MTU and Rolls-Royce creating Turbo-Union. The resulting engine was extremely compact, enabling a relatively small airframe design, and incorporated afterburning for an unprecedented thrust increase of near 50%.

With the Panavia 100 concept extinct, the MRCA authorised for prototyping in 1970 was a two-seat, multi-role aircraft with provision for a range of air-to-air missiles, but when the first prototype completed its maiden flight from Manching on August 14, 1974, it was optimised for air-to-ground work. Nine prototypes and six pre-production aircraft were built, the last of the latter flying almost three years after production had been authorised on March 10, 1976.

Back in 1971, the RAF had, ironically, laid out its plans for a stretched interceptor variant of the MRCA, although the UK's intention to pursue such a development dated back as far as 1969. By the time the first of the pre-production aircraft flew on February 5, 1977, the MRCA had become Tornado, specifically Tornado Interdiction Strike (IDS), since the RAF interceptor had become the Tornado Air Defence Variant (ADV). Featuring minor equipment variations compared to the West German and Italian IDS aircraft, the initial RAF Tornado variant was the GR.Mk 1, which first arrived with the Trinational Tornado Training Establishment (TTTE) at RAF Cottesmore on July 1, 1980.

The TTTE trained aircrew from all three Panavia nations, using relatively small numbers of dual-control aircraft that retained all the capability of their regular counterparts. The RAF's first frontline Tornado squadron exchanged Avro Vulcans for Tornados in 1982. Re-forming at RAF Honington on June 1, No. IX (Bomber) Squadron has remained with the aircraft ever since.

Meanwhile, the Tornado ADV had flown for the first time on October 27, 1979, beginning a long and somewhat troubled test programme for what had become known as the Tornado F.Mk 2. The aircraft's radar caused most concern and the F2s delivered to 229 OCU from November 1984 carried ballast rather than the detection equipment. They were never brought up to full ADV standard, represented by the Tornado F.Mk 3, which formally entered frontline service with 29 Sqn on April 1, 1987.

Over almost 25 years in service, the F.Mk 3 was dramatically upgraded, initially for the 1991 Gulf War, which also saw new systems and capabilities added to the GR.Mk 1. The brief conflict saw the attack Tornado employed in the low-level airfield denial role for which it had been designed, before switching to medium-altitude laser-guided bombing, for which it had not. A handful of aircraft introduced the prototype Thermal Imaging Airborne Laser Designator (TIALD) pod into service before the fighting ended, marking the start of a precision attack capability that has become the Tornado's hallmark.

Since 1991 there has been little relief

Service Operators

Unit	Type	Operational on the GR.Mk 4
IX(B) Sqn	Tornado GR.Mk 4	1999
12(B) Sqn	Tornado GR.Mk 4	2001 & January 9, 2015
31 Sqn	Tornado GR.Mk 4	1999
41(R) TES	Tornado GR.Mk 4	April 1, 2004

from combat operations, with Tornado GR.Mk 1 and F.Mk 3 active in policing and combat missions over the Balkans and Iraq, then back to Iraq in force for Operation Desert Fox in 1998 and Telic, the UK contribution to Operation Iraqi Freedom, in 2003. The GR1 fought alongside the dramatically upgraded Tornado GR.Mk 4 in 2003, the latter bringing true precision capability to the jet and compatibility with the Storm Shadow cruise missile, which 617 Sqn debuted in service during the conflict.

As soon as the GR4 was released from combat over Iraq, it deployed for Operation Herrick, replacing the McDonnell Douglas/BAe Harrier in Afghanistan from 2009. Less than two years later, Tornado Force was simultaneously deploying jets to Kandahar and Italy, for Operation Ellamy over Libya in 2011. Employing Paveway IV and Brimstone in both operations, Tornado exercised precision, low-collateral damage weapons options that remain unique to the RAF.

It also employed the Reconnaissance Airborne Pod Tornado (RAPTOR) system and Litening III targeting pod on intelligence-gathering missions. The Tornado had pioneered digital imaging technologies in its GR.Mk 1A version from December 1986. The variant performed exceptional *Scud*-hunting work during Granby and remained an important tactical reconnaissance asset. Some GR1As were modified to GR.Mk 4A standard, but with the advent of RAPTOR, the reconnaissance capability has since been absorbed into the general Tornado GR4 fleet.

The Tornado also held a dedicated anti-shipping capability, embodied in the GR.Mk 1B in service with 12 (Bomber) Squadron from 1993 and 617 Sqn from 1994. The aircraft was modified to fire the Sea Eagle missile, but the capability fell into abeyance when the GR.Mk 4 programme began.

Since Operation Ellamy, the Tornado Force has drawn down towards the type's planned out of service date (OSD), now set for 2019. The 2010 Strategic Defence and Security Review called for

a reduction in frontline GR4 squadrons to two, but the need to maintain a constant deployment for Operation Shader saw a squadron re-formed and 12(B) Sqn was thus only very briefly disbanded, returning as a third unit.

The GR.Mk 4 has been subject to a constant series of minor upgrades, gradually enhancing its capability so that today's Tornado is very far removed from the jet conceived to meet a multinational requirement during the 1960s. With Tornado's OSD set, Project Centurion is transferring its capabilities, particularly Brimstone and Storm Shadow, to Typhoon. Two new Typhoon squadrons and the incoming Lightning will take over and build upon the tactics and effects that will have been delivered by Tornado in almost four decades of service. ⊙

A lightly-loaded GR4 prepares to depart RAF Marham on a training sortie. Since XV(R) Sqn's disbandment at RAF Lossiemouth on March 31, 2017, Marham has become the centre of RAF Tornado operations. Sgt Nik Howe/© UK MoD Crown Copyright 2017

Shorts Tucano T.Mk 1

Shorts Tucano T.Mk 1	
Powerplant	one 1,150shp Honeywell TPE331-12B turboprop engine
Length	32ft 4¼in (9.86m)
Height	11ft 1¾in (3.40m)
Wingspan	37ft (11.28m)
Wing area	208sqft (19.33m²)
Maximum take-off weight	6,470lb (2,935kg)
Maximum level speed at 10,000ft	277kt (513km/h)
Maximum rate of climb at sea level	3,270ft/min (997m/min)
Range	954nm (1,767km)
Maximum altitude	25,000ft

ROLE: The Tucano T.Mk 1 provides basic fast jet training (BFJT) to RAF and RN aircrew on their training pathway to frontline fast jet aircraft. It is flown by 72(R) Sqn with No. 1 Flying Training School (FTS), at Royal Air Force Linton-on-Ouse.

CAPABILITY: The Tucano T1 combines the economy of turboprop power with jet-like handling and is capable of providing a full range of aircrew training. Formation flying, low-level navigation, poor weather flying and aerobatic handling are taught on 72(R) Sqn, taking advantage of the aircraft's excellent endurance to maximise sortie utility. From its base in North Yorkshire, The Tucano is able to fly training sorties as far away as Wales and central Scotland, finding the most suitable weather and taking advantage of varied training environments.

Service Operators

Unit	Type	Re-formed as Tucano Operator
72(R) Sqn	Tucano T.Mk 1	2002

Service Variants

Designation	First Delivery	Status
Tucano T.Mk 1	June 1988	Operational

Shorts
Tucano

TYPE HISTORY. The search to replace the Cessna T-37 in US service ultimately led, via a rather tortuous route, to the Beechcraft T-6C Texan II, the type scheduled to replace the Tucano in the BJFT role. Ironically, it was the wider T-37 replacement market that also spurred Brazil's Embraer into developing the EMB-312 Tucano, designed against a Força Aérea Brasiliera (FAB, Brazilian Air Force) requirement and first flown on August 16, 1980.

The FAB took its first example in September 1983 and subsequently amassed a sizeable fleet, latterly including the larger and considerably more powerful EMB-314 Super Tucano, a next-generation turboprop trainer that has also seen extensive combat use in the light attack and air-to-air roles. Among its export successes, the Tucano received a large order from France,

which installed its own avionics and, most importantly, the Royal Air Force.

Contemporary RAF basic fast jet training was performed on the Hunting Jet Provost, which had entered service in the 1950s and introduced jet power and a tricycle undercarriage to the basic training regime. Almost three decades later, the Tucano made for a radical change, with its turboprop power and tandem, rather than side-by-side seating. Indeed, it was the first tandem-seat RAF basic trainer to enter service since the de Havilland Canada Chipmunk of 1950.

Various changes were made to the base machine and in order to meet British requirements in the event of a low-level birdstrike the Tucano's canopy was modified; at the same time, it was reprofiled to be closer to that of the Hawk. It was also discovered that the

Tucano's climb rate on the 750hp of its PT6A-25C turboprop was insufficient and the type was re-engined with the considerably more powerful Garrett (now Honeywell) TPE331. Embraer modified one aircraft with the new engine in Brazil, supplying it to Shorts of Belfast in 1986 as a pattern airframe for the 130 licence-built aircraft that followed for the RAF.

Shorts flew the first Tucano T.Mk 1 on December 30, 1986 and the type entered service with the Central Flying School at RAF Scampton, for trials, in June 1988. The first Tucano ab initio course began at RAF Church Fenton with 7 FTS in December 1989. Today, students come to the Tucano from the Tutor and progress onto the Hawk T2, but from 2019 the Tucano will be replaced and the fast jet training progression will be Prefect, Texan II, Hawk T2. ◉

T.Mk 1

The Tucano's rear seat is raised to give the instructor a view over the student's head.
Geoffrey Lee/Planefocus

Grob G 115E
Tutor T.Mk 1

ROLE: Army Air Corps, Fleet Air Arm and Royal Air Force pilots all receive their elementary flying training on the Grob Tutor T.Mk 1. Managed in a pooled fleet arrangement, the Tutor also equips 16 University Air Squadrons (UASs) and 12 Air Experience Flights (AEFs) throughout the UK, providing flying instruction to university students and air experience flying to members of the Air Cadet organisation.

CAPABILITY: The Tutor is ideally simple to fly, yet also sufficiently demanding to be a fine elementary trainer. Its side-by-side seating

Service Variants

Designation	First Delivery	Status
Tutor T.Mk 1	July 15, 1999	Operational

arrangement maximises instructor/student interaction in the air, while its large cockpit canopy provides an excellent outside view for circuit flying.

TYPE HISTORY: First flown in 1985 as an aerobatic sportplane, the Grob G 115 was chosen to replace the Scottish Aviation Bulldog in UAS and AEF service, as well as to equip a

Central Flying School (CFS) squadron, in June 1998. Ninety-nine aircraft were purchased and operated by VT Aerospace with civilian registrations. This system remains in force, with military personnel providing flying instruction and civilian contractors performing maintenance.

The CFS received its first Tutors on September 13, 1999 and the first UAS delivery, to Cambridge UAS, occurred the following day. The all-composite Tutor is named after the 1930s' Avro Tutor basic trainer and remains in widespread service, although its EFT role is being taken over by the Grob Prefect. ⊙

Air Experience Flights

Flight	Station
1	St Athan
2	Boscombe Down
3	Colerne
4	Glasgow Airport
5	Wittering
6	Benson
7	Cranwell
8	Cosford
9	Linton-on-Ouse
10	Woodvale
11	Leeming
12	Leuchars

University Air Squadrons

Squadron	Flying Station
Bristol	Colerne
Cambridge	Wittering
East Midlands	Cranwell
East of Scotland	Leuchars
Liverpool	Woodvale
Manchester and Salford	Woodvale
Northern Ireland	Aldergrove
Northumbria	Leeming
Oxford	Benson
Southampton	Boscombe Down
Birmingham	Cosford
Glasgow and Strathclyde	Glasgow Airport
London	Wittering
Wales	St Athan
Yorkshire	Linton-on-Ouse

Among several operators, the Tutor flies with 57(R) Sqn, based at RAF College Cranwell. Sgt Jack Pritchard/© UK MoD Crown Copyright 2017

Service Operators

Unit	Type	Beginning of Tutor Operations
16(R) Sqn	Tutor T.Mk 1	2008
57(R) Sqn	Tutor T.Mk 1	2008
115(R) Sqn	Tutor T.Mk 1	2008

Specification

Grob Tutor T.Mk 1	
Powerplant	one 180hp Textron Lycoming AE-360-B piston engine
Length	24ft 9in (7.54m)
Height overall	9ft 3in (2.82m)
Wingspan	32ft 9¾in (10m)
Wing area	131.40sqft (12.21m²)
Maximum take-off weight	2,182lb (990kg)
Never exceed speed	185kt (343km/h)
Maximum rate of climb at sea level	909ft/min (277m/min)
Range at 75% power with 45-minute reserves at 4,000ft	446nm (826km)
Maximum altitude	10,000ft

Eurofighter
Typhoon

Typhoon Force is committed to Operation Shader, the ongoing fight against Daesh in Iraq and Syria. This jet was on a combat mission in February. © UK MoD Crown Copyright 2017

Specification

Eurofighter Typhoon FGR.Mk 4	
Powerplant	two Eurojet EJ200 turbofans each rated at 20,000lb st (90kN) with afterburning
Length	52ft 4¼in (15.96m)
Height	17ft 4¼in (5.29m)
Wingspan	36ft 4½in (11.09m)
Wing area	538.20sqft (50m2)
Empty weight	around 22,000lb (10,000kg)
Loaded weight	around 46,300lb (21,000kg)
Maximum speed	Mach 1.8
Brakes off to Mach 1.5 at 35,000ft	less than 2 minutes 30 seconds
Maximum altitude	55,000ft
Armament	internal 27mm Mauser cannon, plus AIM-120 AMRAAM and ASRAAM air-to-air missiles, and Enhanced Paveway II and Paveway IV precision-guided bombs. Future weapons will include the Meteor air-to-air, and Storm Shadow and Brimstone air-to-ground missiles

ROLE: The Typhoon FGR.Mk 4 is a highly capable and extremely agile fourth-generation multi-role combat aircraft, capable of being deployed for the full spectrum of air operations, including air policing, peace support and high-intensity conflict. Initially deployed in the air-to-air role as the Typhoon F.Mk 2, the aircraft now has a potent, precision multi-role capability as the FGR4. The pilot performs many essential functions through the aircraft's hands on throttle and stick (HOTAS) interface which, combined with an advanced cockpit and the Helmet Equipment Assembly (HEA), renders Typhoon superbly equipped for all aspects of air operations.

Although Typhoon has flown precision attack missions in all its combat deployments to date, its most essential role remains the provision of quick reaction alert (QRA) for UK and Falkland Islands airspace. Detachments have also reinforced NATO air defence in the Baltic and Black Sea regions.

CAPABILITY: With its multi-role capability and variety of weapons, the Typhoon FGR4 is capable of engaging numerous target types. In the air-to-air role it employs the infrared-guided Advanced Short Range Air-to-Air Missile (ASRAAM) and radar-guided, beyond visual range Advanced Medium Range Air-to-Air

Missile (AMRAAM). These weapons, used in conjunction with the jet's ECR-90 Captor radar and PIRATE electro-optical targeting system, combine with the Typhoon's superior performance and manoeuvrability to make it a formidable platform.

For ground-attack and close air support (CAS) missions, Typhoon is compatible with the GPS/laser-guided Enhanced Paveway II and Paveway IV weapons, usually in conjunction

with the Litening III targeting pod. Its regular configuration for the armed reconnaissance and CAS roles includes Litening III, Paveway IV and the internal 27mm gun.

Paveway IV offers cockpit-programmable impact angle, impact direction and fuse delay features for precisely tailored target effects. The 27mm gun is ideally suited to providing warning shots or for accurate attacks against targets including light vehicles and personnel.

TYPE HISTORY: In 1979, France, West Germany and the UK embarked upon the European Combat Fighter (ECF) study, which the RAF initially hoped might inform decision making over a replacement for the Harrier and Jaguar. When it subsequently envisaged a secondary air-to-air role for the type, it also became a potential Phantom successor, but the three nations' requirements had diversified and although proposals came from BAe, France's Dassault and West Germany's MBB, there was little common ground.

Meanwhile, the Panavia partner nations, responsible for creating the Tornado, embarked upon an Agile Combat Aircraft (ACA) programme, but this too foundered. Nonetheless, West Germany was now determined that a five-nation consortium, including France, Italy, Spain and the UK, remained the way ahead.

Wishing to press on in some form, in 1983 the British government ordered what was hoped would be a pair of Experimental Aircraft Programme (EAP) demonstrators, optimistically

with input from Italy and West Germany. Such input was not forthcoming and BAe built only one EAP, employing RB.199 engines as used in the Tornado and an advanced aerodynamic configuration. The aircraft was hugely impressive and remarkably close in layout to the machine that eventually emerged as the Eurofighter Typhoon.

Italy, Spain and the UK saw EAP as the basis of a fighter that would satisfy all their requirements, while France pushed for the Dassault ACX concept originally submitted against the ECA

Service Variants

Designation	First Delivery	Status
Typhoon T.Mk 1	December 2003	Upgraded to T3 standard
Typhoon F.Mk 2	December 2003	Upgraded to FGR4 standard
Typhoon T.Mk 3	July 2008	New-build aircraft and upgrades
Typhoon FGR.Mk 4	July 2008	New-build aircraft and upgrades

requirement, and West Germany was keen to keep the five partners together. France decided to go its own way in 1985, eventually maturing ACX into the superlative Rafale, while the remaining nations agreed a specification for a new fighter in December that year.

In September 1987 this became the formal specification for the European Fighter Aircraft (EFA), although huge differences in operational requirement still remained. The Eurofighter consortium of BAe, MBB, Italy's Aeritalia and Spain's CASA was established to develop and

build EFA, receiving a development contract on November 23, 1988; Eurojet was formed to develop a new turbofan engine and EuroRADAR to design the fighter's radar system.

Successfully negotiating the complications expected of an international programme and the challenges of creating any technologically advanced system, Eurofighter flew the initial EFA Demonstrator Aircraft (DA1) for the first time on March 27, 1994. Without radar and powered by RB.199s, this German aircraft (built by DASA, which had by now consumed MBB) enabled a

Top left: **A considerably longer canopy covers the two-seat cockpit of the Typhoon T3. This aircraft was assigned to 41(R) TES for trials.** SAC Cathy Sharples/© UK MoD Crown Copyright 2017

Above: **Although it represents an unlikely operational fit, with four Meteors on the fuselage shoulder hardpoints, ASRAAM on the outer underwing pylons, triple Brimstone launchers inboard, a pair of drop tanks and Paveway IV on the inner wing pylons, this development Typhoon hints at the type's immense capability.** Jamie Hunter/Aviacom

start to test work, an effort fortified on April 6, when BAe's similarly configured DA2 took off for its maiden flight.

Italy's DA3 was next up, on June 4, 1995, built by Alenia (established in 1990 by the merger of Alitalia and Selenia) and equipped with Eurojet EJ200 engines, but still without radar, followed by the first two-seater, Spain's DA6, on August 31, 1996. Alenia flew DA7 on January 27, 1997 and DASA's DA5, the first example built with the ECR-90 radar, on February 24, 1997; back in the UK, BAe had delayed DA4's first flight until March 14, 1997 so the radar could be installed.

With the full development fleet flying, thoughts turned to production. It was decided that the aircraft would be produced in three 'Tranches', each of increasing capability, within which 'Batches' would provide incremental advances in performance through smaller numbers of aircraft built in 'Blocks'. Thus, Tranche 1 was defined as three Batches built as Blocks 1, 2 and 5. In 1998 it had also been determined that the aircraft would be named Typhoon for export customers and the RAF, Tifone by the Italians and Tifón by Spain; it is the EF2000 in German service.

Standing QRA is a permanent, 24/7/365 Typhoon Force commitment. Jets are scrambled in response to aircraft that have lost radio contact, failed to file flight plans or otherwise find themselves in trouble. Sgt Peter George/© UK MoD Crown Copyright 2017

A series of five Instrumented Production Aircraft followed, with Alenia's IPA2 first into the air, on April 5, 2002. By now, DASA had become part of EADS, which flew IPA3 on April 8, followed by BAE Systems (which had absorbed BAe) with IPA1 on April 15, all of them two-seaters. Single-seaters IPA4, built by what was now EADS CASA, and BAE Systems' IPA5 flew on February 27 and June 7, 2004, respectively, paving the way for full production.

Service Entry

In the meantime, Four Nation Type Acceptance had been granted on June 30, 2003, enabling a start to UK-specific testing, in particular with 17 (Reserve) Squadron, the Typhoon Operational Evaluation Unit, which had re-formed at BAE Systems' Warton facility on September 1, 2002 and received its first Typhoon there on December 18, 2003. In September, 29 (Reserve) Squadron also formed at Warton, as the nascent Typhoon operational conversion unit (OCU), with aircraft seen in its distinctive markings from the following May.

Working closely with BAE Systems, these two units prepared the Typhoon, its crews and support personnel for service, both squadrons moving to RAF Coningsby in spring 2005. There the Typhoon frontline began to form on April 1, 2006, when 3 (Fighter) Squadron re-formed as the jet's first operational unit, becoming active three months later.

In service, the initial Tranche 1 aircraft were designated Typhoon T.Mk 1 for the two-seaters and F.Mk 2 for the single-seaters, their equipment fit limiting them to the air defence role, albeit to a level never before seen in UK skies. With this capability, the Typhoon F2 took over responsibility for UK QRA on June 29, 2007.

The Typhoon had been developed and promoted as a 'swing-role' platform, meaning it was equipped with sensors and weapons suitable for multiple roles in a single mission. This complex capability was to be expressed incrementally through the production programme, but with the possibility of a Typhoon deployment under Operation Herrick, the UK added an austere air-to-ground capability to its Tranche 1 jets from 2008, modified aircraft introducing the T.Mk 3 and FGR.Mk 4 designations. Equipped with the Litening III targeting pod and Paveway II laser-guided, or Enhanced Paveway II laser/GPS-guided bombs, these aircraft were ultimately not required in Afghanistan.

While the UK was introducing air-to-ground capability to Tranche 1, BAE Systems had begun delivering Tranche 2 jets to RAF Coningsby. Four of these machines flew to the Falkland Islands, where they relieved the Tornado F3 of its long-standing air defence duties in September 2009.

Capability Enhancement

Typhoon development has continued in carefully executed phases, as was always the intention. This process received additional impetus from Project Centurion, which aims to transfer core Tornado GR4 capability onto Typhoon by the 'Tonka's' 2019 out of service date. Paveway IV has been operational on Tranche 2 Typhoon for sometime, with the completion of Meteor integration next, followed by Storm Shadow and then Brimstone.

Having first deployed into combat for Operation Ellamy (over Libya) in 2011, Typhoon Force began an enduring commitment to Operation Shader (Iraq/Syria) in December 2015. It has also been a regular contributor to the Baltic Air Policing effort under Operation Azotize and most recently bolstered NATO air defence over the Black Sea, deploying four jets to Romania, in addition to the standing commitment of QRA in the UK and Falkland Islands. Most recently, Typhoons deployed to Estonia for air-land integration training with a British Army battle group.

Typhoon Force currently stands at five frontline squadrons, plus the OCU, while 41(R) Test & Evaluation Squadron (TES) operates a small Typhoon fleet under the Air Warfare Centre. Strength is set to expand under the 2015 Strategic Defence and Security Review, however, which made provision for two additional squadrons to be equipped with early-standard aircraft currently held in storage. It seems likely these units will primarily fly air defence and training missions, enabling the existing squadrons to concentrate on the multi-role and attack aspects of Typhoon capability. ◉

In April, 1(F) Sqn deployed Typhoons to the US for Atlantic Trident. The exercise saw them working with and against French Rafales and US Air Force Raptors. Sgt Ralph Merry/© UK MoD Crown Copyright 2017

Above left: **Taking off during Exercise Griffin Strike in 2016, this 11(F) Sqn Typhoon serves to illustrate the type's configuration. The anhedralled foreplanes and squared-off engine air intakes are particularly distinctive.** Sgt Peter George/© UK MoD Crown Copyright 2017

Service Operators

Unit	Type	First Delivery
1(F) Sqn	Typhoon	September 15, 2012
II(AC) Sqn	Typhoon	2015
3(F) Sqn	Typhoon	July 2006
6 Sqn	Typhoon	September 6, 2010
11(F) Sqn	Typhoon	March 29, 2007
29(R) Sqn	Typhoon	2004
41(R) TES	Typhoon	April 2013

Grob G 109B
Vigilant T.Mk 1

The Vigilant motor glider is the least common of the two glider types in RAF service. © UK MoD Crown Copyright 2016

ROLE: The Air Cadet Organisation uses the Grob G 109B motor glider, known in service as the Vigilant T.Mk 1, to provide basic flying and gliding training to its cadets. It is currently employed by 645 Volunteer Gliding Squadron (VGS) at RAF Topcliffe and 631 VGS at RAF Woodvale. They train air cadets in basic flying techniques, ultimately enabling them to fly solo.

The RAF Central Gliding School at RAF Syerston, Nottinghamshire also uses the Vigilant, to train VGS instructors.

CAPABILITY: The Vigilant is a simple motor glider ideally suited to its air cadet training role.

Specification

Grob Vigilant T.Mk 1	
Powerplant	one 95hp Grob 2500E1 piston engine
Length	26ft 7in (8.10m)
Wingspan	57ft 1in (17.40m)
Maximum speed	130kt (241km/h)
Maximum altitude	8,000ft

Grob G 103A
Viking T.Mk 1

The Viking T1 exhibits classic sailplane configuration.
Geoff Parselle/© UK MoD Crown Copyright 2017

ROLE: The Grob G 103A Twin II Acro, known as the Viking T.Mk 1 in service, is used by the Air Cadet organisation to give basic gliding training to air cadets. Nine Volunteer Gliding Squadrons operate the type at locations around the UK, training air cadets to a standard sufficient for them to fly solo. The RAF Central Gliding School at RAF Syerston also uses the Viking, for VGS instructor training.

CAPABILITY: The Viking is capable of high-performance flying and simple aerobatics. A cost-effective modern glider, it is ideally suited to its air cadet training role.

Specification

Grob Vigilant T.Mk 1	
Length	26ft 10in (8.18m)
Wingspan	57ft 5in (17.50m)
Maximum speed	119kt (220km/h)
Maximum altitude	8,000ft

Airbus Defence and Space
A330 MRTT Voyager

The pylons for the refuelling pods under the Voyager's outer wing are mounted to the hardpoints inherited from the A340 wing. On the four-engined airliner they hold the outer engine pylons. LAC Lloyd Horgan/© UK MoD Crown Copyright 2017

ROLE: Voyager replaced the Lockheed TriStar and Vickers VC10 as the RAF's sole air-to-air refuelling (AAR) tanker and also operates as a strategic air transport. The aircraft is in service as the Voyager KC.Mk 2, equipped with two underwing pods for refuelling fast jets, and as the Voyager KC.Mk 3, with an additional centreline hose for use by large aircraft.

CAPABILITY: Fuel offloaded during AAR is taken from the aircraft's standard wing and fuselage tanks, leaving the cabin free for up to 291 personnel and the hold available for freight. As a tanker, capabilities include the ability to operate a 'towline', where the Voyager orbits around a prescribed area awaiting 'receivers', or in a 'trail', where it flies with a number of fast jets, refuelling them over long ranges while taking responsibility for the formation's fuel and navigation.

Service Variants

Designation	First Delivery	Status
Voyager KC.Mk 2	2011	Operational
Voyager KC.Mk 3	2011	Operational

Service Operators

Unit	Type	First Delivery
10 Sqn	Voyager	July 2011
101 Sqn	Voyager	2013

Below: **Voyager supported 6 Sqn's Typhoons for Exercise Red Flag in Nevada during January.** Sgt Neil Bryden/© UK MoD Crown Copyright 2017

AIR TRANSPORT & AIR REFUELLING

A tanker is always on standby to launch in support of the QRA fighters in the UK and on the Falkland Islands, yet Voyager also maintains an ongoing commitment to Operation Shader. This contact with Tornados was over Iraq in April **2016.** © UK MoD Crown Copyright 2017

Specification

Airbus Defence and Space Voyager	
Powerplant	two 71,100lb st (316kN) Rolls-Royce Trent 772B turbofans
Length	192ft 11¾in (58.82m)
Height	57ft ½in (17.39m)
Wingspan	197ft 10in (60.30m)
Wing area	3,892.20sqft (361.60m²)
Maximum speed	around Mach 0.86
Typical mission range	capable of delivering around 132,000lb (60,000kg) of fuel during five hours on station at 500nm (930km) from base
Range with maximum payload	4,500nm (8,334km)
Maximum range with maximum fuel	8,000nm (14,816km)
Maximum altitude	41,000ft
Maximum fuel load	245,000lb (111,000kg)
Maximum payload	around 99,000lb (45,000kg)
Maximum passenger load	291

Alternatively, it can operate as a passenger aircraft in much the same way as a civilian airliner, but delivering personnel safely into theatre thanks to its defensive aids suite. Voyager also offers considerable capacity for the movement of palletised and/or bulk freight in its lower fuselage hold. A versatile aeromedical configuration, including the ability to carry up to 40 stretchers and three critical care patients is available, as is a modest VIP passenger fit.

TYPE HISTORY: Airbus Industrie launched its combined A340/A330 programme on June 5, 1987. It aimed to produce a family of closely related widebody airliners based on the four-engined, long-haul A340 and twin-engined, medium-haul A330. The latter achieved its first flight, with General Electric engines, on November 2, 1992, with the initial Rolls-Royce Trent-powered machine following on January 31, 1994.

Typically for Airbus, the A330's pilots interact with its fly-by-wire system via sidestick controllers rather than the yoke traditionally associated with large aircraft. The basic A330-200 and longer A330-300 have been developed into a wide range of subvariants offering revised performance and different maximum take-off weights.

The earlier A310 widebody had found favour with several air arms as the basis for conversion into a military transport or multi-role tanker transport (MRTT), and Airbus recognised the type's potential as a possible TriStar/VC10 replacement in the early 1990s, trialling a modified aircraft alongside RAF fast jets in 1995.

Above: **The troops aboard this Voyager had just landed at Brize Norton from Afghanistan on December 9, 2013. The type has revolutionised the RAF's ability to more personnel in comfort over extended ranges.** Paul Crouch/© UK MoD Crown Copyright 2017

Right: **Accompanied by a pair of Tornados, this Voyager was over central London for Her Majesty The Queen's official birthday on June 17.** Cpl Neil Chapman/© UK MoD Crown Copyright 2017

It was subsequently expected to offer the A310 MRTT against the UK's Future Strategic Tanker Aircraft (FSTA) requirement, announced as a likely private finance initiative (PFI) programme in 2000. In the event, the procurement process was delayed and although Airbus did not tender, in 2004 the Ministry of Defence announced its intention to acquire a variant of the A330 MRTT.

Under a March 2008 agreement, the AirTanker consortium was selected to provide 14 aircraft under a 27-year contract. This includes a so-called 'Core Fleet' of eight military serialled and one civilian-registered aircraft, supplemented by a 'Surge Fleet' of five civilian-registered aircraft that AirTanker uses commercially to generate additional revenue. The surge aircraft are demodified very close to A330-200 standard and can be recalled for military use if required.

AirTanker owns, manages and maintains the aircraft and provides infrastructure,

support, training facilities and some personnel, in particular Sponsored Reserve pilots and engineers. Named Voyager in service, the A330 MRTT began RAF operations with 10 Sqn on May 12, 2012, flying an air transport sortie from its Brize Norton home base to RAF Akrotiri, Cyprus.

Issues with the drogues, or 'baskets' into which receivers insert their probes during refuelling operations delayed Voyager's debut in the tanker role, but these had been overcome by summer 2013 and the aircraft's ability to deliver fuel to a variety of RAF and allied aircraft expanded very quickly. Also in 2013,

101 Squadron retired the RAF's final VC10s and began flying Voyager alongside 10 Sqn and AirTanker's reservists.

Although it ranges worldwide, Voyager remains home-based at Brize Norton. One aircraft is always available on the Falkland Islands, primarily in support of the Typhoon QRA jets, but also available to the Hercules. Another of the type operates the regular airbridge to and from the Falklands and Voyager is making a major contribution to Operation Shader, offloading fuel to RAF Tornados and Typhoons, and a variety of Coalition jets, including US Marine Corps Harriers and F/A-18 Hornets. ●

Royal Air Force
Aircraft Weapons

Litening III, the dark grey pod on the centreline of the jet rolling away from the camera, is fundamental to both Tornado and Typhoon's precision targeting over the battlefield. Jamie Hunter/Aviacom

Compared to just a decade ago, the Royal Air Force now relies on a relatively small selection of airborne weapons. In that ten-year span, the service has retired the unguided rocket, so long a staple of ground-attack and close air support (CAS), and the unguided, or 'dumb' bomb. Today's attack inventory contains only precision-guided bombs and missiles, while two powerful air-to-air missiles are available to Typhoon Force, with another expected into service next year.

Modern air warfare demands that targets are struck with immense

The Paveway IV GPS/ laser-guided bomb is a primary Tornado and Typhoon weapon. This pair of bombs was under a Tornado, ready for an Operation Shader mission. Cpl Neil Bryden/© UK MoD Crown Copyright 2017

accuracy and crews are expected to use all means necessary to avoid collateral damage; if a target can be left and there is a risk to civilians if it is struck today, then more often than not, RAF crews would rather mark it for tomorrow. The primary means of precision attack is through laser guidance, weapons

homing on laser energy emitted by the Litening III targeting pod carried by Tornado and Typhoon, or from an off-board designator. Where targets are known and weather or visibility restrict the laser's utility, GPS guidance is almost as precise.

Through Brimstone and Paveway IV, the RAF has developed a uniquely capable weapon system for Tornado and one that will also be available to Typhoon from 2018. In that same timescale, Typhoon will also add the Meteor AAM to its armoury, replacing AMRAAM for a quantum leap in air-to-air performance. The ASRAAM/ Meteor combination, in harmony with the jet's internal 27mm cannon and bolstered by planned sensor upgrades, will ensure Typhoon remains a formidable air defender for decades to come. ◉

Aircraft
Weapons

Air-to-Air Missiles:
AIM 120 AMRAAM

The US-designed AIM-120 Advanced Medium Range Air-to-Air Missile (AMRAAM) has been the West's primary medium-range AAM since the early 1990s. It equipped the Tornado F3 and in its latest AIM-120C version will continue as Typhoon's primary medium-range weapon until Meteor replaces it.

AMRAAM homes onto a target identified by the launch aircraft's radar, relying on data from the 'shooter' for guidance and inertial updates until it is close enough to the target to use its own radar seeker, at which point AMRAAM homes autonomously and the launch aircraft is free to turn fully away. The weapon can be launched autonomously against 'pop-up' targets at short ranges.

Typhoon mounts AMRAAM semi-recessed on four underfuselage shoulder hardpoints, for a standard load of four weapons.

User Aircraft

Typhoon

The indented 'trough' to the left of the starboard engine intake on this Typhoon is an AMRAAM station. SAC Mark Parkinson/© UK MoD Crown Copyright 2017

Specification

AIM-120 AMRAAM	
Length	12ft (3.66m)
Diameter	7in (0.18m)
Span	1ft 9in (0.53m)
Weight	346lb (157kg)
Speed	more than Mach 2.5
Range	more than 20nm (37km)
Guidance	Inertial mid-course/active radar terminal

Above: **Launching for a No-Fly Zone enforcement mission early on in Operation Ellamy, this Typhoon carries a typical air-to-air load. The four weapons under its outer wings are ASRAAM, with drop tanks inboard and four AMRAAMs semi-recessed on the fuselage shoulders.** Cpl Babs Robinson/© UK MoD Crown Copyright 2017

AIM-132 ASRAAM

Designed and built in Europe, the AIM-132 Advanced Short-Range Air-to-Air Missile (ASRAAM) was developed to replace the ubiquitous AIM-9 Sidewinder in RAF service and with other air arms. Like the AIM-9 before it, ASRAAM is a heat-seeking or infrared-homing weapon of a type often regarded as a 'dogfight missile'. In fact, ASRAAM's powerful rocket motor and advanced airframe design combine to give it longer range and exceptional manoeuvrability in the closing stages of its flight.

Among the most advanced IR AAMs available, ASRAAM is carried on launch rails attached to the inner wing pylons of Tornado GR4, and under the outer wings of Typhoon, where two weapons under each wing is usual for a common air-to-air fit of four ASRAAM and four AMRAAM. Thanks to its multi-role avionics and sensor fit, Typhoon is able to

User Aircraft

Tornado
Typhoon

Above: **Photographed back in 2006, this 29(R) Sqn Typhoon has ASRAAM under its outer wings.** Geoffrey Lee/Planefocus

Specification

AIM-132 ASRAAM	
Length	9ft 6in (2.90m)
Diameter	6¾in (0.17m)
Weight	192lb (87kg)
Speed	more than Mach 3
Guidance	IR staring array and inertial

combine a mixed AMRAAM/ASRAAM load with a powerful selection of air-to-ground weapons, undertaking air-to-air engagements and attacking surface targets with equal aplomb during the same mission.

Meteor

Developed by MBDA, Meteor is a next-generation AAM capable of extremely long-range engagements against high-speed manoeuvring targets. Ramjet powered, Meteor will reach speeds in excess of Mach 4 and remain under power when it reaches its target.

Like AMRAAM, Meteor is radar guided and relies on updates from the launch aircraft until the target is within range of the missile's own radar. Meteor is a direct replacement for AMRAAM in Typhoon's semi-recessed hardpoints and an April 21, 2017 contract called for its integration onto Lightning. The weapon is due to join Typhoon on the frontline in 2018.

User Aircraft

Lighting – Integration is planned

Typhoon – Integration under way for planned 2018 service entry

Right: **BAE Systems employs this Typhoon on trials, here with Meteor on its forward port and starboard rear positions, albeit slightly obscured by black-and-yellow markings applied for tracking purposes.** Bryan Walsh/ Eurofighter

Specification

Meteor	
Length	12ft ½in (3.67m)
Diameter	7in (0.18m)
Weight	409lb (185kg)
Speed	more than Mach 4
Guidance	Inertial mid-course/active radar terminal

Air-to-Ground Weapons: Brimstone

Brimstone was developed from the US Hellfire air-to-ground missile to provide an advanced anti-armour capability to RAF fast jets. In its original millimetre-wave guided form, the weapon used an internal radar system to find and lock on to vehicle targets. It was used in this mode and fired in salvo by a Tornado formation on at least one Operation Ellamy mission, resulting in widespread destruction of enemy armour.

Given its small size, discrete warhead and accuracy, Brimstone was seen to possess inherent flexibility against a variety of small targets, especially in urban environments where precision and collateral damage concerns are paramount. A semi-active laser guidance system was therefore added to what subsequently became known as Legacy Brimstone, producing Dual-Mode Seeker (DMS) Brimstone.

Like all laser-guided weapons, DMS homes on laser energy reflected from the target and generated either by the launch aircraft (the Litening III pod in the case of Tornado and, very soon, Typhoon) or a designator on the

User Aircraft

Tornado

Typhoon – service entry expected in 2018

Specification

Brimstone	
Length	5ft 11in (1.80m)
Diameter	11¾in (0.30m)
Weight	108lb (49kg)
Speed	more than Mach 1
Range	More than 10nm (18.52km)
Guidance (Legacy)	Millimetric-wave radar
Guidance (DMS)	Millimetric-wave radar/semi-active laser

Above: **DMS Brimstone on a three-round rack fitted to a Tornado GR4.** Sgt Laura Bibby/© UK MoD Crown Copyright 2017

Three Brimstone trials rounds, under a Typhoon. Eurofighter

ground. The result is extremely precise target prosecution, even down to striking small individual installations within a larger facility. The weapon's unique capability was further enhanced when Brimstone 2 entered service on Tornado in 2016.

Brimstone is carried on three-round launchers on the Tornado's underfuselage pylons and will soon be carried underwing on the Typhoon.

GBU-12 Paveway II

The Reaper RPAS employs two US-manufactured weapons, the AGM-114 Hellfire missile and GBU-12 Paveway II laser-guided bomb. In US service parlance, 'Paveway' refers to the type of laser-guidance kit employed, while the alphanumeric designation explains the weapon class and warhead. GBU – Guided Bomb Unit – -12 employs a 500lb Mk 82 warhead. The Paveway

User Aircraft

Reaper

This Reaper took a full warload of four Hellfire and two GBU-12 (the large grey weapons) into combat for a Herrick mission in 2009. POA(Phot) Tam McDonald/© UK MoD Crown Copyright 2017

Specification

GBU-12 Paveway II	
Length	10ft 9in (3.28m)
Diameter	11in (0.28m)
Span	1ft 6in (0.46m)
Weight	800lb (363kg)
Guidance	Semi-active laser

kit includes the seeker head, forward control fins and aft 'wings'.

The launch aircraft or an off-platform designator provides guidance and each Reaper is capable of carrying a pair of bombs, one under each wing.

AGM-114 Hellfire

Alongside GBU-12, Reaper employs the AGM-114 Hellfire missile, in one of its semi-active laser-guided forms. Up to four missiles are carried simultaneously with a pair of GBU-12 bombs, maximising the aircraft's versatility.

User Aircraft

Reaper

Paveway III

Employing the Paveway III laser-guidance and control kit fitted onto a 2,000lb-class warhead, the weapon known only as Paveway III in Royal Air Force service is used against hardened targets, including underground command bunkers and ammunition stores.

User Aircraft

Typhoon

Specification

Paveway III	
Length	14ft 7¼in (4.45m)
Span	3ft ¼in (0.92m)
Weight	2,513lb (1,140kg)
Guidance	Semi-active laser

Enhanced Paveway II & III

While laser-guided weapons provide immense accuracy and rapid engagement solutions against arising targets or targets of opportunity, the designating aircraft must have and be able to maintain sight of the target throughout the guidance process. Cloud, precipitation and battlefield smoke or dust can deny the designator visibility, in which case GPS guidance may be used against known, fixed targets.

The Enhanced Paveway II (1,000lb-class) and Paveway III (2,000lb) weapons combine laser and GPS/inertial guidance, providing crews with the flexibility to engage a range of target types in all weathers, by day or night. In service the weapons are typically known to crews as EPWII and EPWIII, respectively.

User Aircraft

Tornado
Typhoon

Specification

Enhanced Paveway II & III	
Length, EPWII	12ft ¾in (3.68m)
Length, EPWIII	14ft 4¾in (4.39m)
Span, EPWII	1ft 4½in (0.42m)
Span, EPWIII	3ft ¼in (0.92m)
Weight, EPWII:	1,202lb (545kg)
Weight, EPWIII	2,491lb (1,130kg)
Guidance	Semi-active laser/GPS

Paveway IV

Paveway IV was developed specifically to meet a UK requirement for a lightweight GPS/laser-guided bomb of extreme accuracy and posing minimal risk of collateral damage. It employs a 500lb warhead based on the US Mk 82 and is frequently combined with

User Aircraft

Lightning – integration planned
Tornado
Typhoon

Specification

Paveway IV	
Length	10ft 2in (3.10m)
Span	1ft 4½in (0.42m)
Weight	500lb (225kg)
Guidance	Semi-active laser/GPS

Brimstone on the Tornado GR4 to provide a unique capability.

While its dual guidance system enables considerable flexibility, it is Paveway IV's cockpit-selectable characteristics, including multiple fusing options, that are key to its devastating effectiveness. The weapon is carried under the Tornado's fuselage and underwing on Typhoon; it will be integrated onto Lightning for internal carriage in the aircraft's weapon bays, enabling stealthy, precision attack in all weathers, by day and night.

Storm Shadow

Storm Shadow was developed in the late 1990s as a conventionally-armed cruise missile for the Royal Air Force and overseas air arms – it is in French service as the SCALP-EG for example. It became operational on Tornado in 2001 and 617 Sqn debuted it in combat during Operation Telic in 2003. Storm Shadow has subsequently been employed against command and control centres and similar hardened targets in Libya, during Operation Ellamy, and in Operation Shader.

The weapon is launched as much as 300nm from its target, deploying wings and flying autonomously under the power of a small turbofan engine. It finds its way through a process of inertial/GPS navigation and terrain profile matching, where the weapon's sensors compare the terrain overflown with an internal database. Terminal guidance is onto pre-programmed GPS co-ordinates or by imaging infrared, the missile ejecting its nose cone to 'look' for its assigned target, again matching what it 'sees' to an internal database.

Upgrades have ensured that Storm Shadow remains a world-class capability when combined with Tornado GR4 and the weapon will arm Typhoon and Lightning in future.

Deployed to Kandahar in 2014 for Operation Herrick, this II(AC) Sqn Tornado has Paveway IV on its fuselage station, with Brimstone aft. The pod under its outer wing is BOZ. Sgt Ross Tilly/© UK MoD Crown Copyright 2017

This was the first Paveway IV drop from a Typhoon, on November 25, 2014. Note how the weapon's 'pop-out' wings deploy as it clears the aircraft. © UK MoD Crown Copyright 2017

User Aircraft

Lightning – integration planned	
Tornado	
Typhoon – service entry expected in 2018	

Specification

Storm Shadow	
Length	16ft 8¾in (5.10m)
Span	9ft 10in (3m)
Weight	2,866lb (1,300kg)
Speed	Mach 0.8
Range	more than 300nm (556km)
Guidance	Inertial/GPS, optional imaging infrared terminal guidance

Although the trials load on this 41(R) TES Tornado GR4 is unrepresentative of the frontline, it serves to show Storm Shadow's configuration. The jet has BOZ pods on both outboard pylons. Cpl Mark Parkinson/© UK MoD Crown Copyright 2017

Guns: ARD L112A1 General Purpose Machine Gun

The RAF employs the 7.62mm General Purpose Machine Gun (GPMG) – commonly known as the 'Gimpy', pronounced 'Jim-pee' – in its

Air Role Derivative (ARD) L112A1 form. It is used as a 'door gun' on the Puma HC2, enabling the rear crew to deliver suppressive fire from either side of the cabin.

Belt fed and gas operated, the L112A1 differs from the standard GPMG in having a fixed gas regulator and other minor modifications. It is fired from a specific mount, designed to restrict movement and prevent damage to the aircraft. Its cyclical rate of fire is between 600 and 800 rounds per minute.

User Aircraft

Puma	

M60D Machine Gun

The 7.62mm M60D machine gun provides suppressive fire from the Chinook, mounted in either or both of the port forward escape hatch and/or starboard entry door, and/or on the aircraft's rear ramp. As with the GPMG, mechanical stops on the gun mount prevent accidental damage to the helicopter and the weapon is manually fired. Ammunition is expended at up to 550 rounds per minute.

User Aircraft

Chinook	

M134 Minigun

Another Chinook weapon, the 7.62mm M134 Minigun is also fired from the forward escape hatch or entry door. A six-barrelled, electrically driven, percussion-fired weapon, the M134 takes its power from the aircraft's 115V electrical supply.

Using belt-fed ammunition, the M134 fires at up to 4,000 rounds per minute.

User Aircraft

Chinook	

Mauser

Both Tornado and Typhoon feature an internal 27mm Mauser cannon. A high-performance, electrically fired, gas operated weapon, the Mauser fires at 1,000 or 1,700 rounds per minute depending upon cockpit selection.

A WSOp mans the M134 Minigun in a Chinook. SAC Matt Kirwan/© UK MoD Crown Copyright 2017

Its high muzzle velocity and rapid rate of fire create a weapon with considerable hitting power against air and ground targets. In Tornado it is primarily a low-collateral damage strafing weapon for use against soft-skinned vehicles and personnel. Typhoon pilots have the option of engaging ground targets with cannon fire, but may also employ the Mauser against aerial targets, were it could be used as an effective weapon in a close-in engagement or for the delivery of warning shots should a target aircraft refuse to respond to radio calls or hand gestures.

User Aircraft

Tornado	
Typhoon	

Other Stores: BOZ-107

Tornado carries the BOZ-107 chaff and flare-dispensing pod, usually under its starboard outer underwing pylon, although it may also be mounted to port. The system dispenses chaff to confuse enemy radar emitters and flares to defeat heat-seeking missiles, and has been subject to considerable modification and upgrade.

User Aircraft

Tornado	

Litening III

The Litening III targeting pod is primarily used for finding and designating targets for laser-guided weapons, but also generates full motion video (FMV), which may be downlinked to a Remotely Operated Video Enhanced Receiver (ROVER) terminal. ROVER is essentially a

The muzzle of the Mauser cannon can be seen emerging low down on the starboard forward fuselage of this Tornado GR4. The aircraft was deployed for Herrick and also mounts Paveway IV, Brimstone and a Litening III. Sgt Ross Tilly/© UK MoD Crown Copyright 2017

Loaded for a Herrick mission, this Tornado GR4 has an upgraded BOZ-107 pod on its port outer wing pylon. Sgt Ross Tilly/© UK MoD Crown Copyright 2017

User Aircraft

| Tornado |
| Typhoon |

Specification

Litening III	
Length	7ft 2¾in (2.20m)
Diameter	1ft 4¼in (0.41m)
Weight	454lb (206kg)

This still taken from Litening III FMV shows Paveway IVs hitting an arms cache in Libya during Ellamy, in 2011. © UK MoD Crown Copyright 2017

hardened laptop and its use enables personnel on the ground to see what the airborne crew is seeing, in near real time. It enables unprecedented co-operation between Tornado and Typhoon crews and JTACs, for example.

Both Tornado and Typhoon carry Litening III on underfuselage hardpoints, where its field of view is unimpeded by aircraft structures or other stores, and Litening III also enables them to contribute a unique FMV product to ISTAR Force output.

RAPTOR

The Reconnaissance Airborne Pod Tornado (RAPTOR) employs electro-optical and infrared sensors to gather high-resolution imagery that may be viewed in the cockpit, transmitted via data link to the ground in near real time, or collected for download on the aircraft's return to base.

Gathering a vast array of images on every sortie, RAPTOR is typically employed from medium altitudes and stand-off ranges. It proved its capability decisively during Operation Herrick and provided useful intelligence over Nigeria in 2014.

RAPTOR-carrying Tornados have been collecting essential intelligence since the very beginning of Operation Shader and in combination with platforms including Sentinel and Airseeker, the Tornado/RAPTOR continues to make a unique contribution to ISTAR Force.

User Aircraft

| Tornado |

Specification

RAPTOR	
Length	19ft ¼in (5.80m)
Width	2ft 7½in (0.80m)
Weight	2,205lb (1,000kg)

RAPTOR is carried only beneath the fuselage of the Tornado GR4. Cpl Nik Howe/© UK MoD Crown Copyright 2017

Sky Shadow-2/ Common Jamming Pod

The Sky Shadow electronic countermeasures (ECM) pod has been a standard Tornado fit since the aircraft entered service. Usually carried to port, opposite the BOZ-107, Sky Shadow was developed specifically for Tornado and first delivered in 1980. From the outset it was capable of detecting, analysing and jamming enemy radar emissions.

Today's pod looks essentially similar to the 1980s' version, but appearances in this case are misleading. Sky Shadow was initially updated to Sky Shadow-2 configuration, but

User Aircraft

| Tornado |

Launching for an Ellamy mission out of Gioia del Colle, this Typhoon has two underwing drop tanks. It also has a Litening III pod on its centreline and four Paveway II bombs. The latter is now out of service, but similar in appearance to EPWII. Sgt Pete Mobbs/© UK MoD Crown Copyright 2017

was more recently reworked as the Common Jamming Pod (CJP). Developed by Selex, CJP inserts a new suite of digital technology into the Sky Shadow shell. As well as internal electronic systems, it includes a pair of towed radar decoys, similar to those deployable from Typhoon's wing tip pods.

Drop Tanks

Drop tanks, auxiliary external fuel tanks that may be jettisoned if required, are a standard means of increasing a fast jet's range.

Two tank sizes are available to Tornado, holding 1,500 litres (330Imp gal) or 2,250 litres (495Imp gal) of fuel each – they tend to be known in service by their litre capacities. The larger tanks were originally a Tornado F3 fit, but found their way onto the GR1 during the 1991 Gulf War. Tornados typically operate with a pair of either size tank on their inner underwing pylons, but for long-range deployments two 'twenty-two fifties' underwing and a pair of 1,500-litre tanks under the fuselage is a common fit.

Typhoon employs a 1,000-litre (220Imp gal) drop tank, typically carrying one under each wing, although a third may be carried on the centreline. It is not uncommon for training missions to be flown with the single centreline tank in place. ❂

User Aircraft

| Tornado |
| Typhoon |

A 29(R) Sqn Typhoon leaves Coningsby's runway for a training mission, mounting a single drop tank on its centreline. SAC Cathy Sharples/© UK MoD Crown Copyright 2017

Regiment gunners carry a variety of personal equipment, typically including the L85A2 rifle and a sidearm. Ian Forshaw/© UK MoD Crown Copyright 2017

RAF Regiment

The Royal Air Force Regiment takes responsibility for the defence of RAF airfields and assets at home and on deployment. Airpower is often most easily destroyed on the ground and the Regiment therefore plays a key role in the security of aircraft, ground support equipment and personnel, as well as airfield infrastructure.

Force protection is another primary RAF Regiment role. An extension of its wider security function, force protection typically sees small teams of personnel moving with helicopters and providing security at landing zones, or with larger fixed-wing aircraft. A typical scenario in the latter case might see a handful of Regiment troops travelling aboard a Hercules carrying aid into an unstable region. Their role on the ground would be to secure the aircraft and its personnel during the unloading process and then right up to the point of departure.

Regiment forward air controllers from the Air Land Integration Cell at RAF Honington work with a 6 Sqn Typhoon. Sgt Andy Walker/© UK MoD Crown Copyright 2017

The Regiment also provides specialist training and personnel for the tactical air controller role, where ground teams work closely with combat aircraft, directing their attacks against pinpoint and/or highly dynamic targets on the battlefield. Meanwhile, the Regiment's contributions to counter-terrorism activities; chemical, biological, radiological and nuclear defence; and specialist operations are perhaps less well known, but equally important.

Right: Here an L115A3 Long-Range Rifle is combined with the Schmidt & Bender sight. A mesh-like anti-glare shield over the sight's optics prevents reflected light giving the sniper's position away. SAC Phil Dye/© UK MoD Crown Copyright 2017

Far right: The L110A2 Light Machine Gun fires a 5.56mm round. SAC Gary Kearney/© UK MoD Crown Copyright 2017

The Royal Air Force Regiment employs a variety of sidearms, personal weapons, large-calibre machine guns and other ordnance to fulfil its primary combat roles. Gunners engaged in the dismounted close combat role would likely carry a sidearm and personal rifle as a minimum, working in teams to carry larger calibre weapons, mortars or the Javelin anti-tank missile.

Adding to the equipment ensemble, body armour provides essential protection, while a personal radio keeps personnel in touch with their patrol commander. The camouflaged Personal Clothing System includes ammunition and equipment pouches so that reloads and crucial items of kit are easily to hand under fire.

Above: **The Regiment's L131A1 General Service Pistol is based on the Austrian Glock 17.** Stuart Hill/© UK MoD Crown Copyright 2017

Left: **The L111A1 Heavy Machine Gun fires a 12.7mm round.** Cpl Paul Oldfield/© UK MoD Crown Copyright 2017

Royal Air Force Regiment
Weapons

RAF REGIMENT WEAPONS

Javelin is a medium-range fire-and-forget anti-tank weapon. SAC Lee Goddard/© UK MoD Crown Copyright 2017

The L85A2 may also be equipped with the 40mm Underslung Grenade Launcher (UGL), as here. SAC Robyn Stewart/© UK MoD Crown Copyright 2017

Regiment personnel fire an 81mm mortar during Exercise Lions Thunder in 2016. SAC Mark Parkinson/© UK MoD Crown Copyright 2017

Below: The 81mm mortar is a multi-role weapon capable of firing high-explosive ordnance, or of creating illumination or a smoke screen. SAC Tracey Dobson/© UK MoD Crown Copyright 2017

The L129A1 Sharpshooter rifle is based on the Lewis Machine Tools LM07. It includes a telescoping stock and fold-down handgrip. Stuart Hill/© UK MoD Crown Copyright 2017

The L85A2/UGL combination includes a revised sighting arrangement. The UGL has a separate trigger, so the rifle can be fired while a grenade is chambered. SAC Joshua Dines/© UK MoD Crown Copyright 2017

Royal Air Force Regiment
Vehicles

A variety of specialist vehicles provides essential mobility to RAF Regiment squadrons. Heavier machinery includes the Mastiff, essentially a 6x6 armoured truck, plus a variety of protected patrol vehicles, including the Foxhound, Jackal and Panther.

A Jackal vehicle, armed with a Heavy Machine Gun.
Sgt Ross Tilly/© UK MoD Crown Copyright 2017

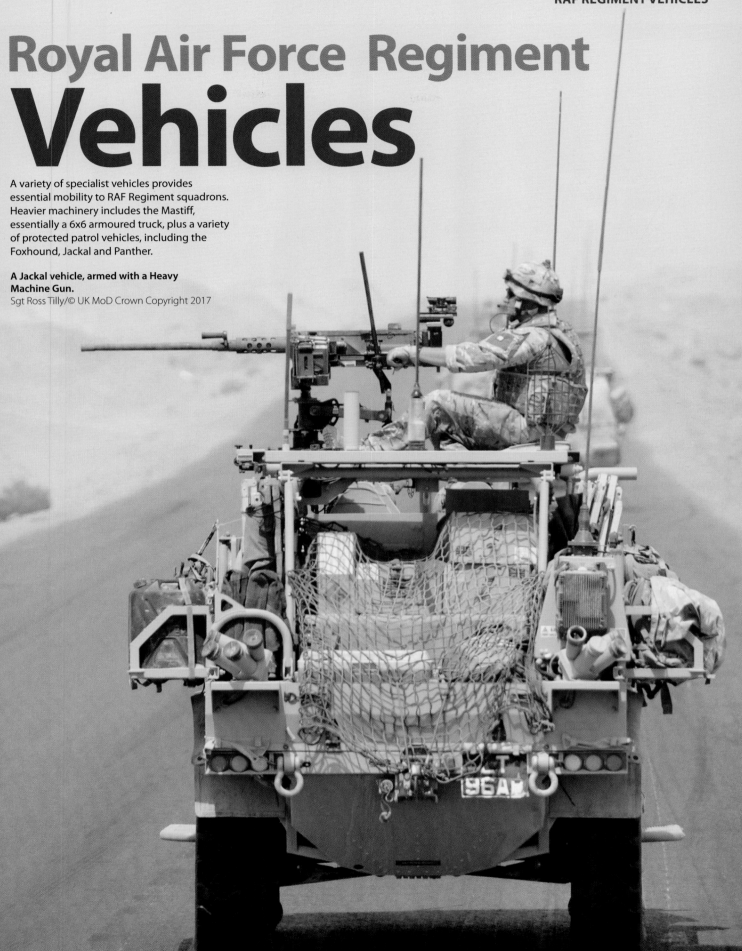

This Foxhound Light Protected Vehicle was patrolling Camp Bastion in 2014. The vehicle is equipped with a 7.62mm GPMG. Sgt Ross Tilly/© UK MoD Crown Copyright 2017

A Panther leads a Jackal in Afghanistan. Sgt Ross Tilly/© UK MoD Crown Copyright 2017

Numbers 15 and 34 Squadrons, RAF Regiment, performed this live-fire exercise with HMG-armed Mastiff vehicles in 2014. Cpl Babs Robinson/© UK MoD Crown Copyright 2017

The Tactical Supply Wing employs the impressive Oshkosh off-road fuel truck to support aircraft in the field. Cpl Rob Travis/© UK MoD Crown Copyright 2017

Royal Air Force
Airfield & Other V

The Atlas 2K is a specialist aircraft loading platform. © UK MoD Crown Copyright 2017

Aircraft tow tractors are essential to aircraft ground mobility. Sgt Andy Benson/© UK MoD Crown Copyright 2017

A plethora of ground vehicles supports day-to-day Royal Air Force operations, some extremely specialised and others commonplace at the world's airports. Among the latter, telescopic loading platforms, including the Atlas and Trepel, are very familiar, but easily overlooked in the excitement of a holiday departure or the busy bustle of Brize Norton. The RAF's aircraft tow tractor fleet and aircraft refuellers might also fit nicely into a civilian airport, but the mighty off-road Oshkosh tanker would almost certainly turn heads.

Among the Service's more specialised equipment, the Oshkosh employs a highly mobile tractor/trailer combination to deliver large quantities of fuel into the field, especially in support of deployed helicopter operations. It's a dramatic vehicle, perhaps only matched in stature by the Rough Terrain Cargo Handler (RTCH, or 'wretch'), an off-road forklift-cum-crane capable of handling a loaded ISO container.

Of course, many of the vehicles populating an RAF station are regular vans, trucks and cars, but in some cases appearances are deceptive. The Mercedes Sprinter vans that serve the Royal Air Force Mountain Rescue Service (MRS) are excellent examples of specialist role adaptations within regular vehicle bodies. All MRS Sprinters are to a 4x4 specification designed and engineered by Mercedes specifically for the Service. Two types of vehicle exist, the standard load carrier and a command, control and communications (C3) variant, equipped for HF, satcom, U/VHF AM/FM, Airwave, mobile and internet connectivity, and featuring a large retractable tent.

Equally familiar externally, but dramatically modified on the inside, the Explosive Ordnance Disposal trucks employed by the RAF's bomb disposal teams contain a battery of equipment, including a control station for the Cutlass remotely controlled vehicle.

Baggage trucks and trailers, familiar to any airline passenger, are commonplace at Brize Norton. Steve Lympany/© UK MoD Crown Copyright 2017

Based at RAF Wittering, 2 Mechanical Transport Squadron employs a variety of specialist military equipment and essentially civilian trucks. Here an RTCH loads a 15-tonne MAN truck with an ISO container. © UK MoD Crown Copyright 2017

Above: **Like the MRS C3 Sprinter, the Explosive Ordnance Disposal truck looks little more than a blue-lighted, liveried commercial vehicle. Inside, however, it's equipped as a control centre for the Cutlass bomb disposal robot.** Cpl Paul Robertshaw/© UK MoD Crown Copyright 2017

Sitting alongside these unusual vehicles, the RAF's road transport fleet includes a large fleet of leased 'white' vehicles, which are almost completely standard. Since they are not owned by the service, they retain civilian number plates, but the trailers they pull are military registered, leading to the unusual situation where a tractor and trailer legally take to British roads with non-matching registration numbers.

Operated primarily by 2 Mechanical Transport Squadron out of RAF Wittering, these white vehicles haul equipment and supplies across the UK and Europe in support of exercises and operations. Their drivers are trained to safely move high-value, delicate equipment, including jet engines and other aircraft components, as well as munitions and fuels.

Below: **A pair of Large Capacity Aircraft Refuellers services Typhoons at RAF Lossiemouth.** Flt Lt Giles Smith/© UK MoD Crown Copyright 2017

The Carmichael MFV2 Florian fire and rescue truck supports RAF operations at home and overseas. © UK MoD Crown Copyright 2017